The Sixth Sense in the Digital Age

Unlocking the Secrets of Intuition and Extra-sensory Perception

James Miller

The Sixth Sense in the Digital Age

The moral right of the author has been asserted
First published by Rockwood Publishing 2023

GRAHAM HODSON
MANUKA
Honey
ONE OF NATURE'S MIRACLES

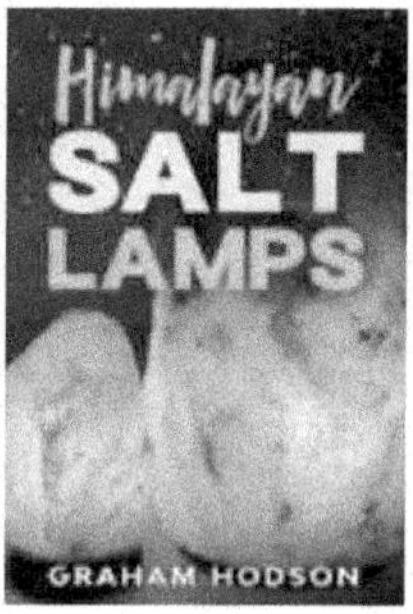
Himalayan
SALT
LAMPS
GRAHAM HODSON

SALT
BLOCK
Cooking
GRAHAM HODSON

SALT
THE EVERYDAY MIRACLE
GRAHAM HODSON

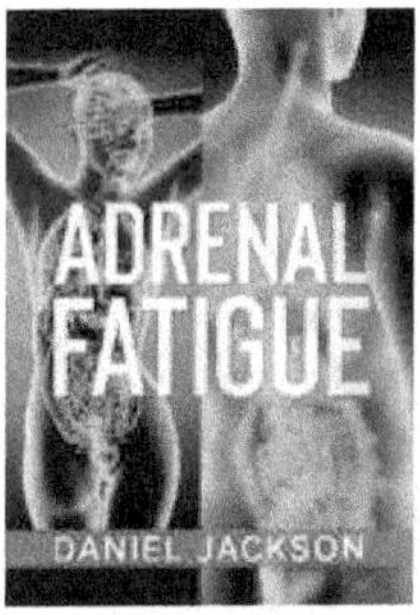
ADRENAL
FATIGUE
DANIEL JACKSON

RED
LIGHT
THERAPY
DANIEL
JACKSON

Digital Detox
AND DIGITAL
MINIMALISM
DANIEL JACKSON

THE PEGAN
Diet
MICHAEL CRAIG

Contents

Chapter 1: The Sixth Sense and Intuition - A Modern Perspective

Defining the Sixth Sense and Intuition

The concept of the 'sixth sense' is as old as human thought itself. Yet, it is far more nuanced than mere folklore or superstition. It encompasses the idea of tapping into a cognitive and perceptual realm that goes beyond the five senses we routinely acknowledge: sight, sound, touch, taste, and smell. Some refer to it as intuition, others consider it psychic awareness, extrasensory perception, or a direct link to the collective unconscious. While the exact nature of this sense may vary from one individual to another, the consensus is clear: there is an additional aspect to human perception that transcends conventional understanding.

In this digital age, we often get so entrapped in data, analytics, and metrics that the intuitive part of us may be neglected, even seen as unreliable or irrelevant. Yet, the successful navigation of our complex world often depends as much on our gut feelings as it does on our logical analysis. The key is to understand this sixth sense better, so we can harness it alongside our other cognitive skills to make more informed decisions, connect more deeply with others, and enhance our personal and professional lives.

Intuition: An Intrinsic Human Trait

Intuition is often described as a gut feeling, a hunch, or an instinct, but such terms merely scratch the surface of this profound phenomenon. In essence, intuition is an innate human trait, an automatic, immediate understanding that arises without the need for conscious reasoning. It draws upon our reservoir of past experiences, learning, knowledge, and instinct, fusing them into an immediate perception that can often guide us when logic falls short.

Scientifically, intuition isn't as mystical or inexplicable as it might sound. It is a form of unconscious cognition, an aspect of our mind that works in the background, constantly processing information, forming patterns, and making connections. When we encounter a situation or problem, our intuitive mind rapidly compares it to this vast store of knowledge, and if it finds a match, it sends a signal - the gut feeling we often talk about.

Intuition, when used correctly, can be a powerful tool. Think of it as a compass, subtly guiding us through life's complexities. It is an ally to logical reasoning, providing insight when information is incomplete, time is of the essence, or the situation is ambiguous. It is by no means infallible, but then, neither is pure logic. The trick is to find a balance between intuition and reasoning, using each where it is most applicable, and combining them when the situation warrants it.

The Sixth Sense: A Perceptive Force Beyond the Physical

Broadly speaking, the sixth sense is a type of extrasensory perception (ESP), a supposed ability to perceive information not gained through the recognized physical senses but sensed with the mind. It can encompass phenomena such as telepathy, clairvoyance, precognition, and mediumship. While such concepts may sound far-fetched or metaphysical, they've been the subject of considerable interest, research, and debate in the realms of psychology and neuroscience for decades.

The sixth sense can be viewed as an extension or amplification of intuition, a further step into the realm of unconscious cognition. While intuition is often based on learned experience and deep-seated knowledge, the sixth sense taps into information that appears to come from outside this realm. Some people describe it as a spiritual or transcendent experience, a connection to a wider consciousness, or an attunement to subtle vibrations in the world around us.

It's worth noting that while the sixth sense and intuition are often intertwined, they are not the same. Intuition tends to be more personal, a direct result of our individual experiences and learning, while the sixth sense is often perceived as tapping into a more collective, universal source of knowledge.

In the upcoming chapters, we will delve deeper into the realms of intuition and the sixth sense, exploring their roles in our lives, their scientific underpinnings, and practical ways to enhance them in the digital age.

Neuroscience of the Sixth Sense and Intuition

At the heart of our understanding of the sixth sense and intuition lies the complex and fascinating world of neuroscience. The human brain, an intricate network of approximately 100 billion neurons, is the powerhouse behind our thoughts, feelings, perceptions, and intuitions. The exploration of its enigmatic mechanisms provides a clearer understanding of these elusive phenomena. So, let's delve into the captivating realm of neuroscience and unveil the curtain that shrouds the sixth sense and intuition.

The biological roots of intuition are deep-seated within our neural framework. Our brains are constantly sifting through an enormous amount of data, most of which we aren't consciously aware of. This cognitive 'heavy-lifting' occurs in the background, processed by our subconscious mind. When a situation arises that requires a decision, our subconscious mind rapidly scans through this vast database of previous experiences, knowledge, and cognitive patterns. If it finds a match or a relevant pattern, it promptly triggers a response, which surfaces to our conscious mind as an intuitive insight or a 'gut feeling.'

This quick, automatic, pattern-recognition process is largely driven by the basal ganglia and the insular cortex, two deep-seated structures within our brain. The basal ganglia play a critical role in emotions, memories, and pattern recognition, whereas the insular cortex, often referred to as the 'fifth lobe' of the brain, integrates emotional and cognitive information. The gut feeling or visceral reaction we often associate with intuition is believed to originate in the insula, which also plays a key role in interoception, our ability to sense the internal state of our body.

The amygdala, another essential structure in the brain, plays a significant role in shaping our intuitive responses. This almond-shaped structure is the brain's emotional processing center, chiefly responsible for fear responses. It has a unique capability to process emotional information and initiate a response before the rational parts of the brain, like the prefrontal cortex, have fully processed the situation. This mechanism is critical in situations where an immediate reaction is necessary, such as in threatening or emergency situations. The intuitive feeling of 'something doesn't feel right' can often be traced back to the rapid, subconscious processing of the amygdala.

So, what about the sixth sense? The neuroscience behind this phenomenon is less straightforward, primarily because the sixth sense encompasses a range of experiences that can be rather subjective and harder to define scientifically. However, there are areas within our brain that seem to be involved in experiences often attributed to the sixth sense.

The pineal gland, for instance, a small, pinecone-shaped structure in the middle of the brain, is often associated with the sixth sense. Known as the 'third eye' in many spiritual traditions, the pineal gland produces melatonin, a hormone that regulates sleep and wake cycles. Some theories suggest it could play a role in modulating consciousness and facilitating access to subtle, non-physical realms of perception.

In recent years, researchers have begun to focus on the role of the anterior cingulate cortex (ACC) and the prefrontal cortex (PFC) in the context of extrasensory perception. The ACC is involved in a wide array of autonomic functions, such as regulating blood pressure and heart rate, and cognitive functions like reward anticipation, decision-making, empathy, and emotion. The PFC, on the other hand, is crucial for executive functions like decision making, personality expression, and moderating social behavior. It is also involved in managing information in working memory.

Studies involving meditation, a practice often associated with increased sixth sense experiences, have shown an increase in activity within the ACC and PFC. This finding hints towards the possibility that enhanced functioning of these areas could facilitate an increased receptiveness to extrasensory information.

Now that we understand a bit about the neuroscience underpinning intuition and the sixth sense, the question arises: how can we harness this knowledge to improve our intuitive abilities and potentially tap into our sixth sense? First and foremost, it's essential to create an environment where your intuition can thrive. This process starts with being present, listening, and being open to your internal experiences. Meditation and mindfulness practices can be beneficial, as they help in tuning out external noise and tuning into our inner voice. Regular meditation has been shown to alter the structure and function of the brain, particularly in areas associated with attention, interoception, and sensory processing, thereby cultivating a fertile ground for intuition to grow.

Practices such as journaling, reflective thinking, and intuitive exercises (like guessing who's calling before you check the caller ID or intuiting what a friend might be feeling) can help strengthen the link between your conscious and subconscious mind. By paying attention to your intuitive hits and checking them against actual outcomes, you can learn to fine-tune your intuitive capabilities.

When it comes to enhancing your sixth sense abilities, it's important to approach it with an open, non-judgmental mindset. Our modern, logical minds are often quick to dismiss experiences that don't fit into the typical sensory framework. However, if you allow yourself the space to entertain and explore these experiences without bias, you might find your perception beginning to expand.

The neuroscience of intuition and the sixth sense offers a fascinating glimpse into the interplay of biology and perception. By acknowledging and exploring these intricate processes within our brains, we can pave the way for a deeper understanding of ourselves and our abilities. This understanding, in turn, equips us with tools to navigate our lives more effectively and authentically in this rapidly changing digital age.

Cultural Perspectives on the Sixth Sense and Intuition

In the intricate tapestry of human societies, intuition and the concept of a 'sixth sense' have found unique expressions and interpretations across cultures. These phenomena, far from being relegated to the realm of the mystical or the supernatural, have often been deeply woven into the fabric of daily life, helping individuals navigate their social landscape and interact with their environment.

Understanding these diverse cultural perspectives not only provides valuable insights into the universality and diversity of human intuition and sixth sense but also offers practical lessons we can integrate into our lives. This exploration can help us strengthen and expand our intuitive faculties, and possibly our extrasensory abilities, regardless of our cultural background.

In Western societies, intuition is often associated with gut feelings or hunches that guide decision-making, particularly when logic and reasoning are insufficient. This perspective draws from the dual-process theory of cognition, a dominant view in Western psychology, which posits two distinct systems for processing information: an intuitive, automatic, fast-thinking system, and a deliberate, analytical, slow-thinking system. Despite this recognition, there's often a cultural preference for the analytical system, and intuitive insights can be sidelined or overlooked.

Contrastingly, many Eastern philosophies place a great deal of emphasis on intuition, viewing it as a form of higher wisdom. In Buddhism and Hinduism, for instance, intuition is often associated with a deep, non-conceptual understanding that arises from meditation and mindfulness practices. It's seen as a path to enlightenment, a way of seeing beyond the illusions of the material world to the ultimate reality.

In indigenous cultures around the world, intuition and the sixth sense often take on a more communal, relational aspect. For example, among the Aboriginal people of Australia, there's a concept known as 'Dadirri,' which translates roughly as 'deep listening.' This practice involves a quiet, receptive awareness, a deep intuition of the surrounding environment, and a connection with the ancestral spirits. It's a way of knowing that goes beyond the individual and ties into the collective wisdom of the community and the land.

African cultures, too, recognize a type of intuitive knowing often linked to ancestral spirits and communal wisdom. In many African societies, dreams and visions are seen as important intuitive channels, providing guidance and insight from the spiritual realm.

Ancestors are considered active members of the community, and their guidance, accessed through intuition and extrasensory perceptions, is valued and sought in important decisions.

These diverse cultural perspectives highlight the importance of intuition and the sixth sense in connecting with others and the environment, decision making, and spiritual growth. But how can we apply these insights to our own lives, particularly in the context of modern, digital societies?

One key lesson is the value of slowing down and tuning into our inner experiences. In our fast-paced, information-saturated world, it's easy to get caught up in the noise and lose touch with our intuitive voice.

Techniques like mindfulness and meditation, inspired by Eastern philosophies, can help us cultivate a quiet, receptive state of mind that allows our intuition to surface.

These practices can also help us manage stress and enhance our overall wellbeing, which in turn can enhance our intuitive abilities.

Learning from indigenous cultures, we can cultivate a more relational form of intuition, one that connects us with others and the world around us. This can involve practices like spending time in nature, engaging in community activities, and nurturing a sense of connection and interdependence. By opening ourselves to the wisdom inherent in these connections, we can deepen our intuitive understanding and navigate our social and environmental landscape with greater ease and insight.

Another valuable practice is to honor and explore our dreams, visions, and imaginative capacities, much as many African societies do. These can provide a rich source of intuitive insight, helping us tap into subconscious wisdom and potentially extrasensory perceptions. Keeping a dream journal, practicing imaginative visualization, or exploring creative outlets like art, music, or dance can help us access and express this intuitive wisdom.

Respecting cultural diversity is crucial when exploring these practices. It's important to approach them with an attitude of learning and open-mindedness, rather than appropriation.

Remember that these practices have emerged from specific cultural contexts, and their meaning and value are intricately tied to these contexts.

Cultural perspectives on intuition and the sixth sense provide a rich tapestry of human understanding and experience.

By exploring and learning from these perspectives, we can enhance our own intuitive abilities, expand our understanding of extrasensory perception, and navigate our modern, digital world with greater insight and wisdom.

By respecting and valuing diversity, we can foster a more inclusive, holistic understanding of these phenomena, one that recognizes their universal significance while honoring their unique cultural expressions.

Chapter 2: The Digital Impact on Human Perception

How Digital Technologies Influence Our Senses

Living in the Digital Age is a truly immersive experience. Our lives are now intertwined with technology in an intricate symbiosis, and digital media forms an increasingly integral part of our daily routines. But as we weave our way through this digital maze, we often don't stop to ponder a fundamental question: how do digital technologies influence our senses, our intuition, and possibly our sixth sense?

In assessing the digital impact on our perceptions, we might consider the example of augmented reality (AR) and virtual reality (VR) technologies. AR enhances our perception of reality by overlaying digital information onto our physical world, while VR transports us into an entirely different, digitally created realm. Both these technologies dramatically expand the range of our perceptual experiences. They present us with new sensory information, create novel scenarios, and craft experiences that our senses would not naturally encounter.

It's not difficult to see how such technologies might influence our intuition. By adding layers of information and offering a variety of perspectives on our surroundings,

AR and VR can stimulate our intuitive faculties to piece together this complex information in a meaningful way. By exposing us to novel scenarios and allowing us to experiment with different responses, these technologies can also train our intuition, fine-tuning our ability to make rapid, effective decisions under unfamiliar circumstances.

But how does this digital immersion influence our sixth sense? While this is a complex and largely unexplored terrain, we could hypothesize a few possibilities. For one, the enriched sensory input provided by AR and VR might stimulate our brain's pattern recognition capabilities, potentially enhancing our sixth sense. Just as our intuitive abilities can be honed by exposure to diverse and complex situations, our sixth sense might also be refined and sharpened by these digital experiences.

Beyond AR and VR, other digital technologies also profoundly influence our senses. Social media platforms, for instance, bombard us with visual, auditory, and textual information, creating a digital cacophony that commands our attention. While these platforms can enhance our global connectedness, they can also clutter our perceptual landscape and make it harder for us to tune into our intuition or sixth sense. The constant stream of information, the demands for immediate responses, and the addictive pull of notifications can distract us from our inner experiences and silence the whisperings of our intuition.

So, how do we navigate this digital world without losing touch with our intuition and sixth sense? One crucial strategy is to balance our digital immersion with periods of digital detox. Regularly unplugging from our digital devices can create space for our intuition to surface and our sixth sense to operate. This can involve setting specific times for device use, taking regular screen breaks, and dedicating certain times of the day or week to being device-free.

Another strategy is to use digital technologies mindfully. This means engaging with these technologies in a conscious, intentional manner, rather than in a habitual or reactive way. It involves tuning into our sensory experiences, noticing how these technologies impact our senses, and making deliberate choices about our digital interactions.

To foster our sixth sense in the digital age, we might also consider integrating digital practices that stimulate our perceptual abilities. This could involve exploring AR and VR technologies, not just for entertainment, but as tools for enhancing our intuition and sixth sense. Playing strategy games, for instance, can hone our pattern recognition abilities and train our intuition. Engaging with immersive storytelling experiences in VR can expose us to new perspectives and deepen our empathic understanding, potentially stimulating our sixth sense.

The digital age presents both challenges and opportunities for our perception, intuition, and sixth sense. Navigating this landscape requires a balance of mindful engagement with digital technologies and periods of digital detox. By taking control of our digital experiences and using these technologies as tools for growth, we can unlock the secrets of intuition and the sixth sense in the digital age.

The Interplay between the Digital World and the Sixth Sense

The Digital Age, with its all-pervasive technology and ceaseless connectivity, has transformed nearly every aspect of our lives. But what about the less tangible aspects of human experience, such as intuition and the sixth sense? Does our constant immersion in the digital world influence these elusive faculties? And if so, how?

The relationship between the digital world and our sixth sense is a complex one. On the one hand, the immense informational wealth the digital world provides can stimulate our minds and broaden our perceptual horizon, potentially feeding and sharpening our intuitive faculties and our sixth sense. On the other hand, the digital noise can overload our cognitive and perceptual systems, potentially drowning out the subtle signals of our sixth sense and muddying our intuitive clarity.

Let's first consider the possible benefits. With a few keystrokes or screen swipes, we can access a staggering amount of information, connect with individuals and communities worldwide, and immerse ourselves in diverse digital environments. This constant exposure to new information, perspectives, and experiences can stimulate our cognitive and perceptual abilities, training our brain to recognize patterns, make connections, and anticipate outcomes more effectively. These are the very abilities that underpin our intuition and possibly our sixth sense.

Moreover, the digital world offers a unique platform for testing and honing our intuitive abilities. For instance, online games and simulations present complex, dynamic environments where we can experiment with different strategies and responses, learning to trust our hunches and make rapid, effective decisions. Social media platforms, too, can serve as a fertile training ground for our intuition, as we navigate the nuances of online interactions, decode the subtleties of digital communication, and anticipate the ebb and flow of online trends.

However, the digital world also presents significant challenges for our intuitive and extrasensory faculties. The onslaught of information, the ceaseless flow of notifications, and the relentless demands for attention can lead to cognitive overload, making it harder for us to discern the subtle signals of our intuition or sixth sense amidst the digital noise. The immediacy and speed of digital interactions can also stifle the incubation period often required for intuitive insights to surface, curtailing the depth and richness of our intuitive experiences.

Additionally, the very immateriality of the digital world can create a disconnect between our bodily experiences and our cognitive processes. This disconnect can hamper our intuition, which often manifests as embodied sensations, such as gut feelings or physical hunches. Our sixth sense, too, might be stifled by this disembodied immersion in the digital world, given that extrasensory perceptions often involve a heightened awareness of our physical environment and bodily sensations.

So how can we navigate the digital world in a way that supports, rather than suppresses, our intuition and sixth sense? A key strategy is mindful digital consumption. This means being fully present in our digital interactions, aware of how they affect our senses and emotions, and conscious of the choices we make online. By engaging with the digital world in a more conscious, intentional way, we can sift through the digital noise and tune into our intuitive and extrasensory signals.

A regular digital detox can also be immensely beneficial. By taking breaks from our devices, we create the space for our intuition and sixth sense to surface and guide us. This can involve setting aside specific times for unplugging, cultivating device-free zones in our homes, or engaging in activities that bring us in touch with our physical environment and our bodily senses, such as nature walks, physical exercise, or mindfulness practices.

Moreover, we can actively use digital technologies to stimulate and refine our intuition and sixth sense. Online games that require strategic thinking, pattern recognition, or rapid decision-making can serve as excellent training grounds for our intuition. Virtual reality experiences that immerse us in rich, diverse sensory environments can stimulate our perceptual abilities and potentially enhance our sixth sense. Even social media platforms, if used mindfully, can offer valuable opportunities for honing our intuitive understanding of human behavior and social dynamics.

The digital world presents both challenges and opportunities for our intuition and sixth sense. By engaging with this world in a mindful, intentional way, by balancing our digital consumption with regular detoxes, and by actively seeking digital experiences that stimulate our intuitive and extrasensory faculties, we can navigate the digital age without losing touch with these vital aspects of our human experience. Indeed, we can turn the digital world into a powerful ally in our quest to unlock the secrets of intuition and the sixth sense.

The Influence of Digital Overload on Intuition

The Digital Age has changed the landscape of our daily lives in so many ways, from how we work and play to how we communicate and connect. But these changes aren't always beneficial. With the positive strides that technology has enabled, there comes a set of new challenges that we need to address and understand. One of the most significant of these challenges is digital overload, and the toll it can take on our intuitive abilities.

Digital overload refers to the sensory and cognitive inundation that comes from excessive exposure to digital technology. With the proliferation of smartphones, tablets, and personal computers, we have constant access to a relentless stream of information and stimuli. From emails, social media feeds, and news alerts to the vast array of online content available, the sheer volume of digital information can become overwhelming. This deluge can disrupt our mental processes, cause stress, and impact our cognitive abilities, including our intuition.

Intuition is our ability to understand and recognize patterns, make decisions, and form insights based on information that isn't fully conscious or explicit. It's the hunch that guides you when information is incomplete, the gut feeling that nudges you toward or away from a decision, or the flash of insight that brings clarity to a complex problem. The intuitive process operates below the level of conscious thought, drawing on a wide range of cognitive abilities, from memory and perception to emotion and embodied cognition.

The state of constant connectivity and the incessant influx of information can undermine these cognitive underpinnings of intuition in several ways. First, digital overload can lead to cognitive fatigue. The human brain is not designed for prolonged periods of intense focus and information processing. When bombarded with an excess of digital stimuli, our cognitive resources become strained, diminishing our ability to recognize patterns, make connections, and generate intuitive insights.

Secondly, the digital world often prioritizes speed over depth, immediacy over incubation. Intuition requires time to consolidate and process information, to allow subconscious connections to form and surface as intuitive hunches or insights. But in the rapid-paced digital environment, this incubation period is often curtailed, limiting the depth and breadth of our intuitive experiences.

Thirdly, digital overload can disrupt our emotional equilibrium. Our emotional state plays a crucial role in intuition, contributing to the gut feelings that often accompany intuitive insights. But the constant stream of digital stimuli can evoke a wide range of emotions, from excitement and curiosity to anxiety and overwhelm, disrupting the emotional clarity that often aids intuitive understanding.

But how do we counteract the impact of digital overload on intuition? Understanding the problem is the first step, but actionable strategies are also needed.

One effective approach is to practice mindful technology use. Be deliberate about how and when you engage with digital media. Create clear boundaries around your digital consumption and be intentional about your online activities. This could mean setting specific times for checking emails or social media, taking regular breaks from screen time, or setting aside quiet periods for reflection and introspection.

Furthermore, engage in activities that allow your intuition to breathe and flourish. This could be anything from meditation and mindfulness exercises, to immersing yourself in nature, or engaging in creative pursuits such as painting or writing. These activities provide a respite from the digital onslaught, enabling your cognitive resources to replenish and your intuition to surface.

Finally, remember that intuition is like a muscle – the more you use it, the stronger it gets. Make a habit of tuning into your intuition, even in the midst of digital distraction. Ask yourself: How do I feel about this? What is my gut telling me? What does my instinct say? By regularly consulting your intuition and giving it space to guide your decisions and actions, you can keep it active and sharp, even in the face of digital overload.

In the modern world, digital overload is an inescapable reality. Yet, with awareness and thoughtful strategies, we can mitigate its impact on our intuitive abilities. By practicing mindful technology use, providing our intuition with the time and space to operate, and making a conscious effort to tune into our intuition regularly, we can navigate the digital world without sacrificing our intuitive power.

Just as the sixth sense was an evolutionary adaptation to our environment, so too can our intuition adapt and thrive in the digital age. With knowledge, mindfulness, and a commitment to nurturing our intuitive faculties, we can turn the challenges of digital overload into opportunities for intuitive growth and resilience.

Chapter 3: Intuition in Decision Making - A Digital Perspective

The Role of Data in Decision-Making

Data has become a cornerstone of decision-making in the digital age. Whether it's a multinational corporation making strategic decisions or an individual deciding what restaurant to dine in, data is playing an increasingly vital role in guiding our choices. However, as the flow of data continues to grow, it is important to remember that data, in itself, is not wisdom. Wisdom, or the ability to make wise decisions, often lies in our ability to integrate data with our intuitive knowledge and insights.

Data-driven decision-making is a process that involves collecting data, analyzing it, and then using the insights derived from the analysis to make decisions. With the advent of sophisticated technologies, we can now collect and process vast amounts of data with relative ease. In the business world, this approach helps companies gain a competitive edge, improve their operations, and better understand their customers. In our personal lives, data can inform everything from our health and fitness routines to our purchasing decisions and travel plans.

While the merits of data-driven decision making are undeniable, it's essential to remember that data only tells part of the story. Data provides quantitative insights, but often, the qualitative aspects of a decision – the elements that can't be easily measured or quantified – are just as important. This is where intuition comes in.

Intuition is a process that synthesizes information and knowledge from various sources, often without our conscious awareness. It includes tacit knowledge – the kind of knowledge that we've acquired through experience but can't necessarily articulate. In decision making, intuition serves as a sort of internal compass, guiding us when the path isn't clear or when the data at hand is insufficient or ambiguous.

In the digital age, the relationship between data and intuition is not an either-or proposition, but rather a dynamic interplay. The key is to find a balance where data informs our decisions, and intuition guides us when data falls short. Integrating data with intuition can create a powerful decision-making tool, one that combines the quantitative rigor of data with the qualitative richness of intuition.

One of the common challenges readers may face in this digital era is the paradox of choice, exacerbated by the abundance of data. It can lead to analysis paralysis, where the sheer volume of available data makes it hard to make a decision. In such cases, learning to rely on your intuition can be a useful strategy. Intuition can help us simplify

complex decisions, cut through the noise, and focus on what's truly important.
Developing this intuitive capacity begins with self-awareness. Pay attention to your gut feelings or hunches and take note of how often they turn out to be accurate. Over time, you will start to trust these intuitive signals more and integrate them into your decision-making process.

Also, consider times when the data is ambiguous or contradictory. These are situations where intuition can be particularly valuable. Intuition is not about ignoring the data but interpreting it in the broader context of your experiences and perspectives.

Embrace uncertainty as an inevitable part of decision-making. Often, waiting for the perfect data set can lead to missed opportunities. Instead, learn to make decisions in the face of uncertainty, using your intuition to guide you when the data is unclear.

Finally, cultivate a mindset of curiosity and continuous learning. In an era of rapid change and disruption, the ability to adapt and learn is more valuable than ever. By staying open to new experiences and perspectives, you can continually feed and refine your intuitive sense.

Data has undeniably changed the landscape of decision-making, offering valuable insights that can guide our choices. But in the complex and often unpredictable world of the digital age, intuition remains a critical part of the decision-making process. By integrating data and intuition, we can make better decisions - decisions that are not only informed by the facts but also guided by our innate wisdom and understanding. The digital age presents a unique opportunity to harness the power of both data and intuition, enabling us to navigate the complexities of the modern world with greater clarity and confidence.

Balancing Intuition with Data-Driven Decisions

The dichotomy between intuition and data-driven decision making can often feel daunting. On one hand, the advent of the digital age brings us into an era of endless information. On the other hand, as human beings, we are wired with a complex cognitive system capable of forming insightful judgements without relying solely on objective data. The challenge that we face in this data-saturated era is learning to balance these two decision-making mechanisms—intuition and data.

Data-driven decisions are grounded in empirical evidence. In an age where information is as accessible as the device in our hands, making decisions purely based on feelings or gut instincts might seem outdated or even irresponsible. Data gives us metrics, benchmarks, and trends. It is quantifiable and replicable, which brings a level of security and predictability to our choices. But data, regardless of how extensive, cannot fully capture the complex dynamics of the human experience. And that's where intuition finds its space.

Intuition, as previously described, is our internal compass, honed over thousands of years of evolution. It is our subconscious mind synthesizing information and experiences to guide us when the path isn't clear. The intuitive process is fast, automatic, and often comes with a significant emotional component. Intuition allows us to make decisions quickly when there's no time for a thorough analysis of data.

However, it's worth noting that intuition is not infallible. Just as data can be misinterpreted, so can our intuition lead us astray. Our intuitions can be influenced by cognitive biases, past traumas, or misleading experiences. Therefore, relying solely on intuition without checking the available data can result in flawed decision-making.

So, how can we navigate this intricate balance between intuition and data-driven decisions in our daily lives? And how can we ensure that we're making the best possible decisions in an age of information overload?

To begin with, we must understand that intuition and data are not opposites, but rather two sides of the same decision-making coin. They complement each other. Data provides us with a broad view of the situation at hand, based on gathered information. Meanwhile, intuition can help us make sense of that data, highlight what's relevant and fill in the gaps that data can't reach. Understanding this interplay is the first step to making better, balanced decisions.

A simple, practical step you could take towards better balancing intuition and data in your decision making is to start practicing 'informed intuition'. This involves gathering and analyzing all the data you can reasonably obtain in a given situation, then letting your intuition guide your final decision. Over time, you will notice a synergy forming between your intuitive sense and the data you collect.

Be aware of the limitations and potential fallibility of both data and intuition. All data is historical and therefore doesn't always predict future outcomes accurately, especially in rapidly changing environments. Similarly, intuition, while often insightful, can be influenced by biases and emotional states. By remaining aware of these limitations, you can better mitigate their impact on your decisions.

Learn to identify the type of decision you're facing. Not all decisions require the same level of analysis or intuitive insight. Some decisions may be better suited to data analysis, such as choosing the most cost-effective supplier for your business. Other decisions, such as hiring the right person for a team, might require more intuition to gauge cultural fit and future potential.

Nurturing your intuitive abilities is also crucial. This could involve practicing mindfulness, meditation, or other activities that encourage introspection and self-awareness. Creating space for quiet reflection can often allow your intuitive insights to surface more clearly.

The digital age, with its constant stream of data and information, doesn't diminish the importance of intuition. Instead, it amplifies the need for it. By integrating data analysis with our intuitive capabilities, we can navigate the complexities of the modern world more effectively.

Balancing intuition with data-driven decisions is not an easy task, but it is an essential skill in our ever-evolving digital era. It allows us to make decisions that are not only backed by empirical evidence but also aligned with our inner wisdom and human experience. This approach to decision making, rooted in both data and intuition, allows us to harness the best of both worlds, leading to more comprehensive, balanced, and effective decisions in the digital age.

Case Studies: Successful Intuition-Based Decisions in the Digital Age

Examining real-life examples can provide compelling insights into how intuition and data intersect in the digital age. These case studies serve to illustrate how individuals and organizations have successfully relied on their intuitive capabilities, even in data-saturated environments.

The first case takes us into the realm of high-stakes decision-making. Let's consider the legendary American investor Warren Buffett. Known for his extraordinary investment acumen, Buffett's approach combines careful analysis with intuitive judgment. He famously looks for companies that he intuitively understands and believes in for the long term, instead of relying only on short-term data trends. His investment in Apple in 2016 is a notable example. While many were skeptical about the tech giant's growth, Buffett saw potential beyond the data. He intuitively recognized the company's unique customer loyalty and the potential for recurring revenue. The decision proved highly beneficial, demonstrating how intuition could guide successful decisions in data-driven fields.

Moving into the technological sphere, let's delve into the story of Netflix. The streaming giant is well-known for its data-driven strategies, using viewer data to make key decisions about content production and marketing. However, one of Netflix's most significant successes came from an intuition-based decision. The decision to produce the hit series "House of Cards" wasn't purely data-driven.

While data showed that users enjoyed political dramas, the final green light for this significant investment came from the executives' intuitive belief in the script and its potential to captivate audiences. The series became a massive success, signaling Netflix's victorious entry into original content production.

Our third case takes us into the world of entrepreneurship with the story of Spanx founder Sara Blakely. She became the youngest self-made female billionaire by trusting her intuition. Sara saw a gap in the market for a different kind of women's shapewear and, trusting her gut, invested her life savings to create a prototype.

Despite the data suggesting a decline in the hosiery market, Blakely's intuition told her that her product would resonate with many women. She was right. Spanx has since become a hugely successful global brand, showcasing how powerful intuitive insights can be, even in the face of contradictory market data.

The final case study comes from the realm of social media—Instagram's pivot from a check-in app (Burbn) to a photo-sharing app. Founders Kevin Systrom and Mike Krieger, faced with modest success and stiff competition, decided to trust their intuition over the prevailing data.

Recognizing that their users were more engaged with the photo-sharing features, they decided to pivot entirely and focus on building a platform dedicated to sharing beautiful images. This intuitive decision paid off spectacularly as Instagram quickly gained popularity and was eventually acquired by Facebook for $1 billion.

Each of these examples demonstrate the significant role intuition can play in decision-making, even in our data-rich digital age. Whether you're an investor analyzing market trends, an executive in a creative industry, an entrepreneur spotting market opportunities, or a tech founder refining your product, these stories underline the enduring power of intuition.

To leverage intuition effectively, similar to the individuals and organizations in these case studies, it's essential to cultivate a strong sense of self-awareness and trust in one's instincts.

Regularly take time to disconnect from the constant flow of digital information and tune in to your thoughts and feelings. Practice mindfulness, spend time in nature, or engage in activities that allow your mind to wander. These moments of quiet introspection can foster intuitive insights.

Remember that intuition and data are not mutually exclusive; instead, they can provide a more holistic view when combined.

Data offers valuable insights into past trends and current situations, while intuition can guide future-oriented decision-making, helping to navigate uncertainty and complexity.

Intuition, when honed and trusted, can be a powerful ally in the digital age. The case studies discussed demonstrate how intuition, even in our data-saturated world, continues to guide some of the most impactful and successful decisions.

By striking a balance between intuition and data, we can navigate the complexities of the digital age more confidently, making decisions that are not only informed but also intuitively aligned with our vision, values, and goals.

Chapter 4: Cultural Perspectives on Intuition

Investigating how different cultures perceive and utilize intuition

Cultural contexts have a significant influence on how individuals perceive and utilize intuition. By exploring this subject from various cultural perspectives, we can better understand the universality of intuition, its diverse interpretations, and applications in different societies.

Starting our journey in the East, we delve into the cultural ethos of countries like India and China. In these regions, intuition has been an integral part of philosophical and spiritual traditions for millennia. For instance, in Indian philosophy, intuition is considered a form of 'prajna' or wisdom, which transcends logical reasoning and empirical understanding. Similarly, in Chinese philosophy, the concept of 'li' relates to understanding the patterns of nature and life intuitively, which is central to Taoism and Confucianism.

Such cultural perspectives often view intuition as a legitimate source of knowledge, with meditation and mindfulness practices aimed at enhancing intuitive abilities. This is in stark contrast to many Western philosophies, which have traditionally placed a higher emphasis on logic and empirical evidence. However, this attitude in the West is gradually changing as research in fields like psychology and cognitive science validate the importance of intuition in decision-making.

Next, we move to Indigenous cultures, such as the Native American tribes and Australian Aborigines, where intuition is interwoven into the societal fabric. These cultures often place great importance on dreams, visions, and the intuitive understanding of nature's signs and patterns. Such intuitive insights are considered sacred, guiding their understanding of the world and their place in it.

In African cultures, intuition often takes on spiritual connotations. In many African societies, intuition is associated with the ancestral wisdom that guides ethical decisions and social behavior. This respect for intuition underlines a communal wisdom that goes beyond individualistic perspectives.

In contemporary Western societies, the perspective on intuition is evolving, influenced by scientific research and the burgeoning interest in Eastern and Indigenous philosophies. There's an increasing acceptance of intuition as a valuable mental resource. Corporations now encourage intuitive decision-making alongside data analysis, while educational institutions are exploring ways to nurture intuition in students.

However, the rise of digital technology and data-driven cultures poses new challenges. In societies flooded with digital information, finding the balance between data-centric decisions and intuition-based choices can be difficult. The digital overload can sometimes drown out the inner voice, making it crucial to create spaces for quiet reflection and intuitive thinking.

Despite these challenges, the cultural shift towards acknowledging intuition's value is evident. From the boardroom to the classroom, the power of intuition is being recognized and harnessed. This shift is a testament to the enduring relevance of intuition, even in our increasingly data-driven world.

How can we nurture our intuition, considering these cultural insights? One way is to cultivate mindfulness and encourage introspection, practices found in Eastern philosophies. Mindfulness can quieten the noise of the external world and allow the intuitive voice to be heard.

Learning from Indigenous cultures, we can pay attention to our dreams and the patterns in nature, treating them as potential sources of intuitive insight. Engaging with arts, as many cultures do to tap into the intuitive mind, can also help. From African drum circles to Japanese Ikebana (art of flower arrangement), creative expressions can open pathways to intuitive understanding.

Respecting and valuing intuitive insights in our daily lives, as many cultures do, can also strengthen our intuitive capabilities. This involves trusting our 'gut feelings' or 'hunches' and incorporating them into our decision-making process, even when they seem to contradict the available data.

The exploration of intuition from various cultural lenses reveals that intuition is a universally human phenomenon, albeit interpreted and utilized in diverse ways. By incorporating these cultural insights into our understanding, we can foster an environment where intuition is recognized, valued, and effectively utilized. This enriched perspective enables us to navigate the complexities of the digital age with a balanced approach that draws on both intuitive wisdom and data-driven insights.

Are there cultural practices or teachings that can help enhance our intuitive abilities?

Each culture, with its wisdom and practices, offers a unique perspective on intuition, often highlighting paths that can be taken to harness and enhance this ability. Cultural practices and teachings provide a variety of tools, methods, and philosophies to guide us towards a better understanding and use of our intuitive powers. By exploring these cultural resources, we can learn how to cultivate and improve our intuitive abilities.

Starting with Eastern philosophies, particularly those from India and China, meditation and mindfulness are two key practices that are believed to enhance intuition. In these cultures, a meditative state is considered a pathway to connect with the intuitive self, allowing us to perceive subtle insights that are often missed in the daily bustle. The teachings of Zen Buddhism, for instance, emphasize Zazen, a type of seated meditation that promotes a state of alertness and openness, allowing intuitive insights to emerge. Regular practice of meditation and mindfulness, thus, can help us better attune to our intuitive selves.

Ancient Indian practices of Yoga and Ayurveda also present a holistic approach to nurturing intuition. Yoga, with its focus on mind-body balance, can help us become more receptive to intuitive signals. Ayurveda, on the other hand, promotes balanced living and diet to maintain a clear and vibrant mind, fostering an environment conducive to intuitive insights.

Indigenous cultures around the world also offer rich teachings to enhance intuition. For example, Native American cultures believe in the concept of 'vision quests' – spiritual journeys into nature, often involving isolation and fasting, to receive intuitive guidance and insights. While not all of us can embark on a full-fledged vision quest, taking regular time off from our digital lives to connect with nature can help quieten the mind and open up intuitive channels.

African tribal cultures place a strong emphasis on community-oriented wisdom and intuition, which is often passed down through generations in the form of stories and proverbs. Engaging with such collective wisdom can offer intuitive insights that go beyond individual understanding. Engaging with folklore, ancestral stories, and cultural wisdom could offer rich resources for intuition.

Among Western practices, the field of psychotherapy has methods that encourage intuitive thinking. Carl Jung, a Swiss psychiatrist, emphasized the importance of integrating conscious and unconscious elements of the mind to achieve 'individuation,' a state of self-realization that is ripe for intuitive insights. Jungian practices like dream analysis and active imagination can be helpful tools in this process.

The arts and creativity are another avenue to enhance intuition. Many cultures use art — music, dance, visual arts — as a form of expression and a pathway to intuitive understanding. Engaging with creative activities can help us bypass logical thinking and tap into the intuitive mind. Whether it's playing an instrument, painting, or dancing, the arts can offer a meditative state that fosters intuition.

Finally, spiritual practices across cultures, from prayer to contemplation, can also be potent enhancers of intuition. By creating a quiet mental space to connect with the spiritual self, these practices can help us become more attuned to the intuitive voice within.

While these practices hail from diverse cultures and contexts, they all share a common theme — slowing down, quietening the mind, and creating mental space for intuitive insights. In our fast-paced, data-saturated digital world, embracing these cultural teachings can offer the balance we need.

By integrating these practices into our lives, we can foster a mental environment that encourages the emergence and recognition of intuition, enabling us to navigate the complexities of the digital age with an enhanced sixth sense.

Chapter 5: Navigating Digital Spaces with the Sixth Sense

Understanding Digital Intuition: Recognizing Patterns and Trends

As we continue our journey through the sixth sense in the digital age, we arrive at an exciting and integral part of our exploration - understanding digital intuition. Digital intuition, a fairly new concept, refers to our innate ability to comprehend and navigate digital spaces by recognizing patterns, trends, and the underlying algorithms at play. It is our 'gut feeling' in the digital realm that helps us make decisions and choices in the face of immense online information.

In a world where digital technologies permeate our lives, understanding how our intuition adapts to these environments is essential. There's an entire layer of intuitive sense-making that we engage in while interacting with digital interfaces, whether it's deciding which search result to click on, intuitively sensing the credibility of a social media post, or even knowing when a text message doesn't quite capture the sentiment it's supposed to convey.

So, how do we recognize patterns and trends in digital spaces? It starts with paying attention to our digital behaviors and reactions. Do you find yourself always clicking on certain types of headlines? Do you tend to follow suggestions made by your streaming platform? Do you trust certain sources of information more than others? These are clues that our intuitive mind is at work, guiding our actions based on patterns it has recognized over time.

As our interactions with digital interfaces become more frequent and complex, our mind forms associations and understands the digital 'cause and effect.' For example, you may start recognizing that articles from a particular source are often clickbait, or that a certain type of email usually signifies spam. This pattern recognition forms the basis of our digital intuition.

Understanding and nurturing digital intuition involves actively engaging with these patterns, questioning their validity, and refining our reactions. It's a continuous learning process where our intuition becomes sharper with every interaction.

One way to enhance this learning process is by conscious reflection. After an online session, take a moment to reflect on your actions and decisions. What guided them? Did your intuition play a role? Were you satisfied with the outcome? This introspection can help you become more attuned to your digital intuition.

Another crucial aspect of digital intuition involves understanding the algorithms that power our digital experiences. We must remember that these algorithms are designed to capture and retain our attention. Being aware of this fact can enable us to question the suggestions they provide, helping us make decisions that align better with our needs rather than simply following the digital pathway laid out for us.

In essence, understanding digital intuition is about mastering the art of balance. On one hand, we need to harness our inherent intuitive abilities to navigate digital spaces efficiently. On the other, we must be vigilant and question the patterns, trends, and algorithmic decisions to ensure our digital behaviors align with our authentic selves. As we become better at recognizing patterns and trends, we can create a more harmonious relationship between our intuition and the digital world. It's an exciting journey, and as you get better at recognizing the subtle interplay of intuition and digital spaces, you'll find yourself becoming a more empowered and intuitive digital citizen.

Developing a Sixth Sense for Cybersecurity: Spotting Scams and Threats

As we dive deeper into the digital age, our lives are becoming increasingly interwoven with the digital world. With this integration comes the growing risk of cyber threats and scams that can disrupt our online experiences. This brings us to the realm of cybersecurity, where our sixth sense, our intuition, plays a critical role. So, how can we develop a sixth sense for cybersecurity and equip ourselves to spot scams and threats?

The first step to developing a digital sixth sense for cybersecurity is understanding the landscape of cyber threats. These threats can range from phishing emails that attempt to trick you into revealing personal information, to malicious software that can compromise your computer's security. It's important to stay informed about these common cyber threats and how they operate.

However, knowledge alone is not enough. This is where intuition comes into play. Have you ever received an email and felt something was off, even if you couldn't pinpoint what? That feeling is your intuition at work. It's an innate understanding that something is not as it seems. Your intuitive mind is picking up on subtle cues and inconsistencies that your conscious mind may not notice immediately.

Developing this intuitive sense for cybersecurity involves honing in on these feelings of discomfort and uncertainty. When you encounter something suspicious, take a moment to analyze the situation. Why does it feel off? What details are causing this feeling? This process not only validates your intuitive feelings but also helps you understand the specific signs of cyber threats, making it easier to spot them in the future.

But how do you sharpen this intuitive sense for spotting scams and threats? Practice is key. Like any other skill, your ability to intuitively sense cyber threats improves over time, with repeated exposure and conscious awareness.

Take phishing emails, for example. These often have tell-tale signs such as generic greetings, spelling and grammar mistakes, and urgent calls to action. As you encounter more of these, your intuition gets better at picking up on these signs, often alerting you to the threat before your conscious mind has even processed it.

Moreover, it's crucial to create a mental pause before acting on any digital request. This pause gives your intuitive mind the space to consider the information at hand and flag any potential issues. Think before you click, especially when the request involves sharing personal information or downloading files.

Another part of developing a sixth sense for cybersecurity involves understanding the emotional tactics used by cybercriminals. Scammers often prey on our emotions, creating a sense of urgency or fear to push us into acting without thinking. Recognizing when our emotions are being manipulated can help us step back and evaluate the situation objectively, strengthening our intuitive defense against scams.

Finally, remember that intuition in the digital world doesn't operate in isolation. It works in tandem with rational analysis and knowledge. Stay informed about the latest cybersecurity threats and safety measures. This knowledge forms the basis on which your intuition operates, allowing it to spot inconsistencies and threats more effectively.

Developing a sixth sense for cybersecurity is an ongoing journey, and it's okay to make mistakes along the way. Every mistake is a learning opportunity that refines your intuitive abilities. In a digital world filled with potential threats, the ability to intuitively spot scams and threats is an invaluable skill, offering a powerful defense in safeguarding your digital life.

As we cultivate this digital sixth sense, we are not just defending against the immediate cyber threats, but we are also preparing ourselves for the evolving digital landscape. The threats of today may change, but the ability to intuitively sense danger and respond effectively will remain a constant ally, offering us protection in the uncharted territories of the digital world. This skill, like our intuition, is fluid and adaptive, growing with us as we continue to explore the digital age with curiosity and caution.

Digital Empathy: Understanding Others Online

Empathy is an innate human capacity that allows us to comprehend and share the feelings of others. It is a fundamental aspect of human interaction, fostering connection, understanding, and mutual respect. In the digital age, where interactions increasingly occur online, the concept of empathy transcends physical spaces, and we encounter a new realm: digital empathy.

Digital empathy is the ability to empathize with others in online environments. This may seem challenging given the lack of physical cues, which traditionally facilitate empathy. However, it is not only possible but also increasingly critical in our technologically interwoven world. But how can we understand and empathize with others online?

Understanding others online begins with recognizing the human behind the screen. Each user is a person, complete with emotions, experiences, and perspectives. Each post, message, or comment is an extension of this individual. Approaching digital interactions with this mindset can set the stage for empathy.

Then comes the crucial task of active listening, or in this case, active reading. This involves paying close attention to what others say and how they express themselves. Emotions often leak into our digital expressions, whether through word choice, punctuation, emojis, or the content shared. Interpreting these signals can give you insights into others' emotional states, fostering empathy.

However, the digital world can sometimes amplify negative emotions, leading to misunderstandings or conflicts. In such cases, digital empathy calls for restraint and understanding. Before reacting, take a moment to consider the other person's perspective. Could there be external factors influencing their behavior? Is it possible that their words were misinterpreted? This empathetic pause can prevent unnecessary conflicts and promote healthier digital interactions.

Empathy online also encompasses respect for differing opinions. The internet is a melting pot of diverse views, and disagreements are inevitable. However, empathy means respecting others' right to their opinion, even if it doesn't align with yours. Instead of resorting to online arguments, seek to understand their viewpoint. This doesn't mean you have to agree, but understanding promotes empathy and respect, making online spaces more harmonious.

Moreover, digital empathy also involves being aware of and respecting digital boundaries. Just like physical boundaries, digital boundaries vary among individuals. Some may be comfortable sharing personal experiences online, while others prefer to keep certain aspects of their lives private. Respecting these boundaries is a fundamental part of digital empathy.

But digital empathy is not just about understanding others; it's also about expressing your empathy in a way that translates well in digital spaces. This might involve using empathetic language, sharing supportive content, or simply offering a virtual shoulder to lean on when someone is going through a tough time. It's about making the digital world a little more humane, one interaction at a time.

However, cultivating digital empathy is not just a personal responsibility; it's a collective one. Social platforms, digital communities, and organizations all play a role in fostering digital empathy. This could involve creating guidelines for respectful communication, providing tools to report inappropriate behavior, or hosting events that encourage empathetic interactions. Digital empathy is a collective effort that shapes the digital world we share.

Lastly, it's essential to mention that digital empathy should not come at the cost of one's wellbeing. Digital fatigue, a feeling of exhaustion from excessive digital interaction, can hinder your ability to empathize with others. It's crucial to take regular digital detoxes, stepping away from screens to recharge. Balancing online and offline experiences can help maintain your capacity for digital empathy.

By embracing digital empathy, we can navigate online spaces with greater understanding and respect, creating a more inclusive, understanding digital world. It's a testament to our capacity to adapt our innate empathetic abilities to new environments, ensuring that even as we advance technologically, our fundamental human connections remain strong. The digital world, with all its complexities and opportunities, offers a new space for us to extend our empathy and understanding, reaffirming the importance of these traits in the fabric of human interaction. So, let's embrace digital empathy, bringing humanity and connection into the heart of our digital age.

Chapter 6: Training Your Intuition in the Digital World

Recognizing and Trusting Your Digital Intuition

As we sail further into the digital age, our interactions with the virtual world become more integrated with our everyday lives. It's an era where technology plays a key role in every facet of our existence. One aspect that has found a place in this new digital landscape is our intuition, the deep-seated instinctive compass that guides us. This chapter will navigate the pathway to recognizing and trusting what we can call "digital intuition."

Just as with traditional intuition in the physical world, digital intuition also involves sensing patterns, interpreting cues, and drawing on past experiences. However, digital intuition differs in the nature of the input it processes. Instead of tangible environmental cues, it interprets signals in the digital environment, like email content, social media posts, website designs, or even the rhythm of coding languages.

So, how can one develop this elusive digital intuition?

The first step towards honifying digital intuition lies in building a robust understanding of the digital landscape. Familiarize yourself with common online communication styles, trending topics, technology advancements, cybersecurity risks, and digital culture. The more knowledgeable you are about the digital world, the better equipped you'll be to identify patterns and anomalies intuitively.

Building your digital intuition is not unlike tuning a musical instrument; it takes practice, attention, and fine adjustments. Spend time exploring various digital platforms, and pay attention to what feels natural and what seems jarring or unusual. Remember, intuition often manifests as a gut feeling, an instinct that something feels right or wrong without a conscious reason.

Also, listen to your feelings of unease. Digital intuition can help protect you from online scams, fake news, or malicious software. If something feels off about an email or a website, don't ignore it. Your intuition might be picking up on subtle cues that your conscious mind hasn't identified yet. In these instances, trusting your digital intuition can be crucial.

Just as we recall physical experiences and learn from them, storing digital experiences is equally important. When you encounter a new situation online, your mind will draw on these stored experiences. If you've ever clicked on a link that turned out to be spam, your digital intuition develops from that encounter, making you more alert to similar future threats.

Don't be disheartened if your intuition leads you astray sometimes. Missteps are part of the learning process. Even the most intuitive people make mistakes. The key is to analyze where your intuition went wrong and adjust it accordingly, refining its accuracy over time.

Another crucial aspect of digital intuition is understanding its limits. In the virtual world, where information can be manipulated, intuition must be used in tandem with critical thinking. It's not about completely trusting every instinct but learning when to rely on intuition and when to lean into logical reasoning. Digital intuition should complement, not replace, rational analysis.

Practice makes perfect, and the same goes for sharpening your digital intuition. Engage in digital activities that challenge your intuitive instincts, such as online gaming, virtual reality experiences, or coding puzzles. These activities offer opportunities to hone your instinctive responses in a digital environment, further developing your digital intuition.

The process of recognizing and trusting your digital intuition is a journey of self-discovery, requiring patience and practice. As we continue to navigate the digital age, this new form of intuition will inevitably become an integral part of our interaction with the virtual world. By fostering this innate capability, we can enhance our digital interactions, staying ahead of risks and making the most of the opportunities the digital world has to offer.

In the grand design of our digital future, your intuition can be a compass guiding you through the sea of information, helping you steer clear of dangers, and leading you towards rewarding experiences. So venture forth, trust your instincts, and let your digital intuition guide you through the fascinating landscape of the digital world.

Exercises for Enhancing Intuition in Digital Spaces

As we delve deeper into the digital age, honing our intuition in digital spaces becomes vital for thriving in this new environment. It's essential not only for navigating digital landscapes effectively but also for guarding against potential risks. Here we will outline several exercises designed to enhance your digital intuition, offering practical guidance and solutions for our readers to overcome common challenges they might encounter online.

The first exercise is **mindful browsing**. This practice is built on the principles of mindfulness, applied to digital interactions. Start by dedicating a specific period to browse the internet, visit various websites, or interact on social media platforms. As you navigate these spaces, pay close attention to your thoughts and feelings. How does the content you encounter make you feel? What instinctive reactions do you have towards the things you see? Over time, mindful browsing can heighten your awareness of your digital intuition, allowing you to recognize it more readily.

Next is the **trust-distrust game**. This exercise is designed to refine your instinctual judgment about the trustworthiness of digital content. Select a few websites or social media profiles and instinctively categorize them as trustworthy or untrustworthy based on your initial gut feeling. Once you've made your instinctive judgment, validate it with research. Were your instincts correct? This exercise can enhance your digital intuition over time by reinforcing correct judgments and learning from the incorrect ones.

Another valuable exercise is the **pattern recognition challenge**. The digital world is rife with patterns, from user behaviors to the algorithms powering your search engine. Start by picking a theme or concept. This could be something like how people react to certain posts on social media or how a particular search engine ranks various sites. Try to intuitively identify patterns or trends. Afterward, compare your intuitive insights with actual data or expert analysis. This exercise will help to fine-tune your intuitive understanding of digital patterns and trends.

One fascinating exercise is **intuitive coding**. If you have basic knowledge of any programming language, try this. Start with a simple project and rely heavily on your intuition while solving problems or debugging. As you advance, gradually undertake more complex projects.

Even if your intuition leads you astray, the process of correcting and learning will further sharpen your digital intuition.

Incorporate **meditation and relaxation techniques** into your routine as well. It's well documented that stress can hinder our intuition. Digital spaces, with their constant flow of information and interactions, can be stress-inducing. Regularly taking time to quiet your mind and relax can help maintain a mental environment where your intuition can flourish.

Lastly, the **reflection and journaling** exercise can be of immense benefit. Dedicate some time each day to reflect on your digital interactions and experiences. Did you have any instinctual feelings or reactions? Were they accurate? Keeping a journal of these reflections can help you track your progress over time, identify areas for improvement, and reinforce your understanding of how your digital intuition works.

Embarking on this journey of honing your digital intuition is like learning a new language. It's a language that doesn't rely on words but on instinctual understanding and intuitive insights. It's the language of the digital age, the language of the future. As you practice these exercises, remember that patience and consistency are key. Your digital intuition, like any skill, needs time to develop and grow. Embrace this journey with an open mind and a willingness to learn, and let your enhanced digital intuition guide you through the ever-evolving landscape of the digital age.

Mitigating Digital Overwhelm to Clear Intuitive Pathways

In the realm of the digital age, we often find ourselves inundated with a constant stream of information. Emails, social media updates, news articles, digital advertisements – the flow seems endless, resulting in a common phenomenon known as digital overwhelm. This state of information overload can clutter our minds, impeding the clear intuitive pathways that are essential for effectively navigating the digital world. In this section, we will provide insights into mitigating digital overwhelm and propose several strategies that can be employed to clear these intuitive pathways.

The first and perhaps most crucial step is to acknowledge that digital overwhelm is not an inevitability but a manageable condition. Accepting this can empower us to take the necessary actions to regulate our digital consumption effectively. It involves understanding our digital habits, discerning the beneficial from the detrimental, and making conscious choices about our digital engagement.

A pivotal part of mitigating digital overwhelm involves setting boundaries. Just as we need boundaries in our interpersonal relationships, we also need them in our relationship with the digital world. Establishing and maintaining a healthy digital diet can have a profound impact on our mental well-being and intuitive clarity. This could mean setting specific times for checking emails and social media, taking regular digital detoxes, or even implementing apps that limit screen time. These boundaries are not intended to disconnect us from the digital world but to foster a healthier, more balanced interaction with it.

Intentionality is another powerful tool in our arsenal against digital overwhelm. Rather than aimlessly browsing the internet, we should approach our digital activities with clear intent. Know what you want to achieve from each digital interaction, whether it's seeking information, connecting with others, or simply entertainment. Being purposeful in our digital engagement can help prevent mindless scrolling and the consequent digital overwhelm.

Creating a clutter-free digital environment can significantly reduce digital overwhelm. This includes regularly cleaning up your email inbox, decluttering your digital files, and organizing your digital workspace. Consider it akin to cleaning a physical space. A clean, organized space – whether digital or physical – fosters a calm mind and clear intuition.

Prioritizing quality over quantity in our digital consumption is another effective approach. Instead of trying to read every news article, watch every trending video, or follow every popular influencer, focus on consuming content that genuinely adds value to your life. Choose reliable news sources, follow influencers who inspire you, and engage with digital content that enriches your knowledge and understanding. This selective approach can mitigate digital overwhelm and enhance the quality of your digital experiences.

Another important aspect to consider is managing our emotional responses to digital content. The digital world can evoke a myriad of emotions – from joy to anger, from amusement to sadness. Being aware of these emotional responses and learning to navigate them effectively can prevent digital overwhelm from amplifying these emotions and cluttering our intuitive pathways.

This involves recognizing when certain content is inducing stress or negative emotions and taking appropriate actions, such as taking a break, using stress management techniques, or even seeking support if needed.

Finally, incorporating mindfulness practices into our digital activities can significantly aid in mitigating digital overwhelm. Mindfulness can create a mental space where we can observe our digital activities and their impacts on our thoughts and emotions without getting entangled in them.

This detached observation allows for a clearer understanding of our digital behaviors, empowering us to make more conscious and intuitive choices in the digital space.

Addressing digital overwhelm is not a one-time effort but an ongoing process. It requires continuous self-awareness, regular adjustments, and the willingness to make conscious choices in our digital engagement.

As we clear the clutter of digital overwhelm, we pave the way for our digital intuition to shine through, guiding us intuitively in the digital realm.

Remember that our intuitive abilities are not lost in the digital world – they are there, waiting to be tapped into, waiting to guide us through the complex, exciting, and ever-evolving landscape of the digital age.

Chapter 7: The Sixth Sense, Intuition, and Artificial Intelligence

Understanding Artificial Intuition

The digital age has ushered us into a new era of technology, most notably marked by the advent of Artificial Intelligence (AI). This innovative technology has transformed nearly every aspect of our lives, leading us to question what it means to be truly intuitive. Can machines possess intuition? Is it possible to create an artificial version of the human sixth sense? Let's dive deeper into these questions and explore the intriguing concept of artificial intuition.

Artificial Intelligence has been an area of growing interest, with technological advancements allowing us to create machines that can mimic human cognition. Machine Learning, a subset of AI, allows machines to learn from data and make predictions or decisions without being explicitly programmed to do so. This concept aligns closely with human intuition, which essentially involves making decisions based on prior experiences and subconscious information processing.

However, it's important to distinguish between the functionality of AI and the complexity of human intuition.

Human intuition is a product of the conscious and unconscious mind, shaped by our personal experiences, emotions, and even our cultural and societal influences. It involves a level of understanding and processing that goes beyond mere pattern recognition or data analysis. It's deeply connected to our individuality and our ability to understand and perceive the world around us.

On the other hand, AI, including those equipped with machine learning capabilities, operates fundamentally on algorithms and statistical models. It recognizes patterns and makes predictions based on pre-existing data. Although this may give an impression of 'intuition', it's crucial to understand that these predictions lack the depth and context of human intuition. For example, a machine can predict that a person might buy a certain product based on their past purchases, but it doesn't truly understand why the person made those choices.

The term 'artificial intuition' has been coined to describe AI systems' ability to make fast, accurate decisions based on large volumes of data. This concept is most often used in the field of cybersecurity, where AI systems analyze patterns and behaviors to identify potential threats. However, this 'artificial intuition' doesn't equate to the multifaceted, humanistic nature of true intuition. It lacks emotional perception, personal experiences, and the innate understanding of human behavior that forms the core of our intuitive processes.

While it's fascinating to explore the idea of artificial intuition, it's also essential to consider the implications. One critical concern is the ethical dilemma that arises from entrusting decisions, particularly those with significant consequences, to AI. Given that AI's 'intuition' is based on patterns and data analysis, there's a risk of bias, inaccuracies, or oversights. Moreover, decisions taken without a genuine understanding of human emotions and contexts may lead to undesirable or even harmful outcomes.

Artificial intuition may be an exciting frontier in AI, but it remains a concept in progress, and it's far from replicating the depth and complexity of human intuition. So, where does this leave us in our quest to understand and enhance our sixth sense in the digital age?

This exploration underlines the unique value of our innate human intuition, reinforcing the idea that our intuitive abilities give us a competitive edge - a blend of emotion, cognition, and experience that AI is far from replicating. As we navigate through the digital age, it becomes increasingly essential to harness these intuitive capabilities, allowing us to interact with technology in a way that is thoughtful, conscious, and truly human.

In this digital age, as we interact more and more with AI and similar technologies, we should see them not as replacements for our human faculties, but as tools to augment them. AI can help us sift through vast amounts of information and spot patterns, but it's our human intuition that provides the depth, context, and emotional understanding to these findings. By combining the strengths of artificial and human intuition, we can navigate the digital world with greater insight and wisdom.

So, while we push the boundaries of technology and venture into the realm of artificial intuition, let's not lose sight of the remarkable capacities of our human intuition. Let's continue to nurture this innate ability, for it holds the key to our success and fulfillment in an increasingly digital world.

Can Machines Develop a Sixth Sense?

As we delve deeper into the realm of AI and machine learning, one question that often surfaces is whether machines can develop a sixth sense. Can they perceive beyond the five senses, understanding the subtleties and complexities of intuition? Or, in more precise terms, can AI capture, analyze, and act upon data in a way that mirrors the intuitive decision-making process of humans? In this section, we aim to examine these questions in depth, providing a comprehensive exploration of the potential for machines to develop a semblance of the sixth sense.

To frame this discussion, it's important to understand what we mean by a 'sixth sense'. Traditionally, this term has been used to describe the ability to perceive beyond the five basic senses - sight, hearing, taste, smell, and touch. In a more abstract sense, the sixth sense is often associated with intuition - the ability to understand something instinctively, without the need for conscious reasoning.

In the context of machines, however, the concept of a 'sixth sense' takes on a different dimension. Machines, by design, are devoid of human sensory perception. They don't see, hear, smell, taste, or touch in the way we do. Instead, they gather information through data inputs, which can be processed to provide a form of understanding. As such, when we talk about machines developing a sixth sense, we're essentially discussing the capacity for AI to mimic human intuition - to process data inputs in a way that allows for intuitive, predictive decision-making.

The advent of machine learning and deep learning has brought us closer to this reality. Machine learning algorithms can identify patterns in vast amounts of data, using these insights to make predictive decisions. This capacity for pattern recognition and prediction is, in many ways, analogous to human intuition. We subconsciously analyze patterns based on our experiences and use these insights to inform our future decisions.

Deep learning takes this one step further by mimicking the neural network structure of the human brain. Deep learning algorithms can process data inputs through multiple layers of artificial neurons, each of which can apply a different set of calculations to the data. This allows for a more nuanced understanding of complex data, enabling the machine to make highly accurate predictions.

While these technological advancements suggest machines are capable of a form of 'sixth sense', it's crucial to remember that machine intuition is fundamentally different from human intuition. Machines lack emotional intelligence and the capacity to understand and interpret human experience. They can analyze data and identify patterns, but they cannot truly 'understand' in the way humans do.

This leads us to the concept of 'artificial empathy', a controversial idea in the world of AI. Some believe that machines could eventually be designed to recognize and respond appropriately to human emotions. However, while machines may be able to mimic empathetic responses based on data inputs, it's debatable whether this truly constitutes empathy. Empathy is a deeply human characteristic, rooted in our capacity to share and understand the experiences of others. It's difficult to envisage how this could be authentically replicated in a machine.

Moreover, it's worth considering whether we'd want machines to develop a sixth sense. The ethical implications are profound. If machines were able to mimic human intuition and empathy, how would this affect our relationship with technology? Would we become overly reliant on machines, risking a loss of our own intuitive capabilities? Would machines with a sixth sense be granted the same rights and responsibilities as humans? These questions are as philosophical as they are technological, and they warrant careful consideration.

In light of these discussions, it's clear that machines are making strides towards mimicking human intuition. However, there are limits to what machines can achieve, and important ethical considerations to take into account. As we continue to navigate the digital age, it's essential that we balance our pursuit of technological innovation with a respect for the uniquely human capabilities that machines cannot replicate.

While the idea of machines developing a sixth sense is fascinating, we must remember that our human intuition - our true sixth sense - is an invaluable asset. Our ability to make intuitive decisions, guided by emotion and personal experience, is something machines cannot replicate. In the rapidly advancing digital world, it's more important than ever that we nurture this innate capacity. After all, it's our humanity - our intuition, our empathy, our understanding - that sets us apart in a world of machines.

Ethical Implications of Machine Intuition

In the digital era, machines are developing capabilities that mimic human intuition, leading us to confront a novel set of ethical dilemmas. Machine intuition, a concept that refers to the capacity of AI to predictively process information, forces us to reckon with questions about the bounds of artificial intelligence, the essence of human intuition, and the implications of blurred lines between the two. As we move forward, it is necessary to navigate these uncertainties and shape a future where machine intuition serves to complement human capabilities, rather than overshadow them.

Human intuition, fundamentally, stems from our lived experiences, emotional intelligence, and subconscious processing of information. Our instincts help us in making decisions, often in situations where we lack complete information or time to analyze all the details.

We interpret subtle cues, connect dots based on prior experiences, and sometimes even experience gut feelings that guide our actions. While cognitive science has helped us understand this to some extent, the complexity and depth of human intuition make it a concept that is not fully understood.

Machines, on the other hand, are devoid of emotional experiences or subconscious thought processes. They operate based on algorithms, processing vast amounts of data at high speeds, and generating outputs based on predefined rules and patterns in the data.

With advances in machine learning and deep learning, machines have been successful in pattern recognition, predictive analysis, and decision-making, which could be considered a semblance of intuition.

However, the evolution of machine intuition brings with it a range of ethical considerations that we need to address. Firstly, there's the matter of trust. While AI can improve efficiency and make accurate predictions, over-reliance on machines could erode our human instincts. If we entrust machines with decisions in critical areas such as healthcare, law, or autonomous driving, we are essentially placing blind faith in their 'intuition'.

But without human oversight, any failure or mistake could have severe implications.

The second concern is that of bias. Machine learning models learn from the data they are fed. If this data reflects societal biases, machines can end up perpetuating these biases. While this is not an issue of intuition per se, it becomes critical when we start trusting the 'intuition' of machines. Without careful oversight, machine intuition could become a vehicle for systematic discrimination or bias, undermining fairness and equality.

Thirdly, there's the potential dehumanization of interpersonal interactions. If machines begin to replicate human intuition, we risk creating a world where machine-mediated interactions replace human ones.

As a society, we have to think deeply about whether this is a world we want to live in. Human intuition is inherently tied to empathy, connection, and shared experiences. If we allow machines to take over this space, we risk losing these fundamental aspects of human relationships.

Furthermore, we must consider the implications of AI transparency. As machine learning models become more complex, their decision-making process becomes less interpretable, often referred to as the 'black box' problem.

If we trust the intuitive capabilities of these machines, it becomes crucial to understand how they arrive at certain decisions. Without this, accountability becomes a challenge, and it becomes easy to shift blame onto machines when things go wrong.

Lastly, there's the concern of data privacy. Machine intuition is reliant on data. As AI systems become more advanced, they will require more data to function effectively. This raises questions about data collection, consent, and privacy. We must ensure that the development of machine intuition does not come at the cost of individual privacy rights.

As we navigate these ethical quandaries, it becomes clear that regulating machine intuition will be a complex task. It will require multi-stakeholder collaboration, involving policymakers, technologists, ethicists, and society at large.

We need to develop guidelines that protect individual rights, ensure accountability, and prevent misuse, all while allowing room for technological innovation.

Ultimately, it's about striking a balance. Machine intuition holds significant promise in improving efficiency and enabling us to make sense of complex datasets. However, it should not replace our own intuition or undermine our human capabilities. As we explore the potential of machine intuition, we must simultaneously invest in nurturing our human intuition, empathy, and emotional intelligence.

It's a path fraught with challenges and uncertainties, but it also opens up unprecedented opportunities for growth and innovation. By approaching it with thoughtfulness, foresight, and a firm commitment to ethical principles, we can ensure that the rise of machine intuition serves to enhance, rather than erode, our human experience.

Chapter 8: Enhancing Real-World Intuition in a Digital Age

Importance of Face-to-Face Interactions for Intuition Development

In a digital era where virtual interactions are increasingly the norm, the importance of face-to-face connections for intuition development cannot be understated. While digital communication has undeniably opened a universe of accessibility and instant connection, it is important to remember the irreplaceable value that physical, face-to-face interactions have in shaping our intuitive abilities.

Intuition, a subconscious process relying on the ability to read subtle signals and patterns, is most effectively developed through direct, in-person interactions. This is because face-to-face interactions offer a rich array of sensory information — visual cues, vocal tone, body language, immediate emotional responses — that digital communications often lack. It's the tilt of a head while saying something, the quick flash of expression that speaks volumes, or the underlying emotion in a voice's timbre — these intuitive data points are gathered most effectively in real-time, in-person interactions.

This isn't to suggest that intuition cannot be developed or used in the digital realm. On the contrary, as we've explored in previous chapters, digital intuition is a valuable skill in today's world. However, the depth and complexity of information available in face-to-face interactions give a boost to intuitive development that digital spaces can't quite match.

Consider empathy, an element deeply intertwined with intuition. Empathy often hinges on our ability to perceive, understand, and connect with the emotions of others. In face-to-face interactions, empathetic connections are forged not just through words but through shared experiences, eye contact, and mutual understanding. This process of 'feeling into' another person is much more challenging when physical presence is removed from the equation.

Moreover, face-to-face interactions can challenge and hone our intuitive abilities. They demand a level of presence and immediate response that digital communication often does not. In the physical world, you can't hide behind a screen, craft your responses with ample time, or control how others perceive you to the same extent as in the digital world. This can be an excellent training ground for intuition, pushing you to trust and act on your intuitive hunches in real-time.

In an age where digital and physical worlds are increasingly intertwined, it is essential to see them not as opposing forces but as complementary aspects of our lives.

Embracing the strengths of each, understanding their limitations, and learning how to adapt our intuitive capabilities across these spaces are crucial steps towards developing robust, effective intuition in the digital age. As the subsequent sections of this chapter will further elucidate, grounding ourselves in physical reality and balancing digital and physical inputs play a significant role in fostering a well-rounded intuitive ability.

Techniques for Grounding in the Physical World

While digital technologies are here to stay and continue to transform our lives in significant ways, we need to acknowledge and preserve the vital connection with the physical world. Grounding is a powerful process to bring your focus back to the here and now, anchoring your presence firmly in the physical realm. This practice can sharpen your sensory awareness, deepen your intuition, and enhance overall well-being.

Let's embark on an exploration of how to cultivate grounding techniques to fortify our connection to the physical world and our own bodies.

Mindfulness and Meditation
Mindfulness and meditation serve as the foundational practices for grounding. They train your brain to be present, helping you attune to the sensations of the physical world.

Mindfulness involves paying active, open attention to the present moment. This can mean focusing on your breath, noticing the sensation of sunlight on your skin, or feeling the texture of the earth under your feet. It is a simple yet profound practice that pulls us out from the whirlpool of digital distractions and helps to center ourselves in our physical existence.

Meditation, a deep form of mindfulness, requires dedicated time and space. Regular practice can enhance your capacity for attention and awareness. Whether you choose guided meditations, mindfulness-based stress reduction, transcendental meditation, or any other form, the key is consistency.

Spending Time in Nature

Immersing oneself in nature has a grounding effect. It could be a walk in the park, gardening, hiking in the mountains, or just sitting under a tree. Engaging with nature brings us closer to the earth, quiets our minds, and heightens our senses. The sounds of nature – bird songs, rustling leaves, flowing water – all work as natural stress relievers.

Physical Exercise and Body Awareness

Physical exercises such as yoga, tai chi, dance, or any form of workout you enjoy, are excellent grounding techniques. They promote body awareness, improve focus, and foster a strong connection between the mind and body. When we are physically active, we tend to become more mindful of our bodies' movements and sensations, enhancing our intuition about our own well-being.

Creative Expression

Engaging in creative activities like painting, sculpting, knitting, cooking, or playing a musical instrument is another way to ground ourselves. These activities require a deep engagement that leaves little room for digital distractions. They anchor us in the moment, allowing us to express and release emotions, contributing to a heightened sense of intuition.

Breathing Techniques

Breathing techniques, also known as pranayama in yoga, can be an instant grounding tool. By focusing your attention on the breath, you create a bridge between your conscious and unconscious mind, facilitating intuition.

Grounding Visualizations

Visualization techniques are effective for grounding. One common method involves picturing yourself as a tree. Imagine roots growing from your feet into the earth, anchoring you firmly. Visualize energy flowing from the earth, up through your roots, nourishing you. This visualization not only helps ground you but can also aid in energy regulation.

In the end, grounding in the physical world is a multifaceted and deeply personal practice. The right combination of techniques will differ for each person and may evolve over time. It is important to explore, experiment, and find the strategies that resonate with you. Remember, grounding is not an attempt to escape or devalue the digital world but a means to balance and harmonize our existence across physical and digital spaces. This balance is essential for our mental, emotional, and physical well-being, and serves as the bedrock for developing and nurturing our intuitive abilities.

As we increasingly embrace digital technologies and cultivate digital intuition, these grounding techniques serve as our compass, reminding us of our intrinsic connection to the physical world. In this dance between the physical and the digital, we will find our intuition evolving, resonating with the rhythm of this modern, interconnected reality. It is this balanced and harmonious existence that enables us to unlock the secrets of intuition and extra-sensory perception in the digital age.

Balancing Digital and Physical Inputs to Foster Intuition

Striking a balance between digital and physical inputs is an art, akin to walking a tightrope. Too much focus on either side can lead to an imbalance, affecting not just our mental and emotional well-being but also our intuitive abilities.

In this digital age, it's easy to find ourselves being excessively drawn to our digital devices. Emails, social media, news, and entertainment are all within the reach of our fingertips, providing us with a constant stream of digital input. However, it is essential to balance these digital inputs with physical world experiences to foster intuition. Let's delve deeper into how this balance can be achieved and sustained.

Developing Awareness of Digital Consumption

The first step in balancing digital and physical inputs is understanding your digital consumption. The omnipresence of digital devices has led many of us to spend a significant portion of our waking hours online, often without us realizing the extent of it.

Digital technologies offer myriad benefits, but they can also lead to a sense of being overwhelmed. It's important to recognize when your digital usage is leaning towards excessive or compulsive. Various tools and applications can track your screen time, providing insights into how much time you're spending on different apps and platforms. This awareness is the starting point in understanding how much digital input you're receiving and how it might be affecting your overall balance.

Creating Digital-Free Zones and Times

Once you've gained awareness of your digital consumption, it's time to set boundaries. Establish digital-free zones in your home, such as the dining room or bedroom, where you consciously choose not to use digital devices.

Similarly, setting aside specific digital-free times, like the first hour after waking up or the last hour before bed, can help you disconnect from the digital world and reconnect with the physical world. You could use this time for meditation, reading a physical book, or simply observing your surroundings. These moments of disconnection can provide a necessary pause, helping you tune into your senses and intuition.

Prioritizing Real-Life Social Interactions

While digital communication tools have enabled us to connect with people worldwide, they shouldn't replace real-life social interactions. Face-to-face interactions involve numerous subtle cues such as body language, voice inflection, and eye contact, which are essential in fostering intuitive skills.

By prioritizing real-life social interactions, we can improve our emotional intelligence, empathy, and intuition, all of which can be challenging to cultivate in purely digital interactions.

Practicing Mindfulness in Digital Interactions

Even while using digital platforms, one can practice mindfulness. It means fully immersing yourself in the task at hand, whether it's writing an email, participating in an online meeting, or browsing social media. By being mindful, you allow yourself to use your intuition to guide your digital interactions. This practice can help mitigate digital overwhelm and keep your intuitive channels open.

Balancing Passive Consumption with Active Creation

Another approach to balance digital and physical inputs is to ensure you're not just consuming information passively but also engaging in active creation. It's easy to get lost in an endless cycle of scrolling through news feeds, reading articles, or watching videos.

Balance this passive consumption with active creation, which can be writing a blog post, creating a piece of art, making a home-cooked meal, or building a physical object. Active creation engages different parts of our brain, promotes mindfulness, and provides opportunities for intuitive insights.

Fostering a Strong Physical Connection

While managing digital inputs is crucial, it is equally important to cultivate a strong connection with the physical world. Regular exercise, spending time in nature, practicing mindfulness, and engaging in sensory experiences all contribute to this. These activities ground us, help us tune into our physical bodies, and foster our intuition.

Balancing digital and physical inputs isn't about demonizing technology or romanticizing a life devoid of digital influences. Rather, it's about finding a harmonious balance where we leverage the best of both worlds. The goal is to use digital tools as aids to enhance our lives, not let them dictate our lives.

As we navigate this balance, we open the door to a more intuitive way of living, embracing the digital age without losing touch with our inherent sixth sense. We allow the digital and physical worlds to coexist, interweave, and enrich our life tapestry, and in this balanced existence, we find our intuition not just surviving, but thriving.

Chapter 9: The Future of the Sixth Sense and Intuition in a Digital World

Preparing for a Future Where Digital and Physical Intuition Coexist

As we journey into the uncharted territory of the future, one thing remains clear: our sixth sense and intuition will continue to play an essential role in our lives, even as digital technologies advance at a breakneck pace. While this might feel like a brave new world, it is one where our inherent human abilities and digital tools can coexist and complement each other.

For many, the future brings images of artificially intelligent robots, sophisticated algorithms predicting our every move, and virtual realities that blur the line between the digital and physical world. But amidst these high-tech predictions, we must not overlook the importance of our innate human intuition, that unquantifiable 'sixth sense' that guides us in ways that logic and data often cannot.

So, how do we prepare for a future where digital and physical intuition coexist? How do we ensure that our inherent, intuitive capabilities not only survive but also thrive in this digital age?

Firstly, we must accept and acknowledge that our intuition has a place in this digital world. As we've explored throughout this book, our intuitive abilities are not relics of the past to be discarded in the face of digital progress; rather, they are invaluable tools that can help us navigate this ever-evolving landscape.

Embracing a future where digital and physical intuition coexist starts with understanding the unique value that both bring. Digital technologies, with their vast data-crunching capabilities, can provide us with insights and information at an unprecedented scale and speed. But our intuition, with its ability to tap into subconscious patterns and emotional cues, can offer nuanced understanding and insight that digital tools simply can't replicate. By leveraging both, we can make more informed, balanced decisions.

Next, we need to consciously cultivate our intuitive abilities. In a world increasingly swamped with data and digital input, it's easy to let our logical, analytical minds take the wheel. However, we must create the space for our intuition to shine. Whether it's through meditation, mindfulness practices, spending time in nature, or simply quietening our minds amidst the digital noise, we must actively nurture our intuitive skills.

On a broader societal level, we must advocate for the integration of intuitive learning in our education systems. Just as we teach children mathematics and science, we should also impart the value of intuition. Encouraging the development of intuitive skills from an early age can help foster a generation that's adept at navigating both the physical and digital realms intuitively.

The future also invites us to reconsider how we design and use digital technologies. As we've seen, certain digital practices can hinder our intuitive abilities. Moving forward, we should strive to develop and utilize technology in ways that support, rather than suppress, our intuition. For example, incorporating elements of mindfulness into digital platforms, or creating technologies that encourage real-world social interactions, can help maintain a healthy balance between digital and physical intuition.

Finally, we must remember that at the heart of this future vision is a profound respect for our humanity. In a world where technology is often seen as the panacea for our problems, we must not lose sight of our inherent human abilities. Our intuition, our sixth sense, is part of what makes us human. And as we march towards the future, it's these human qualities, in harmony with digital technologies, that will guide us on the path of true progress.

As we peer into the horizon, we see a future that's not just digital, but also deeply human. It's a future where our ancient, intuitive wisdom dances gracefully with cutting-edge digital tools. It's a future where the digital and the physical, the analytical and the intuitive, don't exist as separate entities but as interwoven threads of the same fabric. This is the future of intuition in the digital age – a future that we can all prepare for, embrace, and shape, starting now.

Lifelong Learning and Adaptation: Key to Navigating the Future

As we ponder about the future, one thing becomes quite clear: The digital age is an era of unprecedented change and acceleration. With technological advancements and evolving digital landscapes, the world around us is transforming at a breathtaking pace. As we move deeper into this digital age, the ability to continually learn, adapt, and embrace new skills and perspectives will be of paramount importance in not just thriving but also making sense of the world around us.

One might wonder: How does one ensure lifelong learning and adaptation in a rapidly changing world? How do we equip ourselves with the tools and mindset necessary to navigate the unchartered territories of the future?

At the heart of lifelong learning and adaptation is an unquenchable curiosity, an eagerness to explore, and an openness to change. Curiosity prompts us to question, to probe deeper, to venture beyond the known into the realm of possibilities. It encourages us to continually seek out new knowledge and experiences, thus fueling our lifelong learning journey.

However, this curiosity and passion for learning must be balanced with the flexibility and resilience to adapt. As the digital age continually reshapes our world, we must be willing and able to adjust our sails, to pivot when needed, and to embrace new ways of thinking and doing. Adaptation, therefore, is not just about learning new skills but also about unlearning and relearning.

Our intuition plays a critical role in this journey of lifelong learning and adaptation. As we've explored throughout this book, intuition is our internal compass, our inner guidance system that can help us navigate the complexities and uncertainties of the digital age. By tapping into our intuitive insights, we can make sense of new information, discern patterns and connections, and make informed decisions in an increasingly complex world.

Moreover, fostering our intuition allows us to go beyond the surface-level knowledge and gain a deeper, more holistic understanding of the world around us. In a digital age characterized by information overload, our intuition can help us sift through the noise and uncover the essential truths. It can guide us in identifying what is truly worth learning and retaining.

Maintaining our intuition in a digital age, however, is not without its challenges. The constant bombardment of digital stimuli can sometimes overshadow our intuitive voices. Hence, it is vital that we consciously create spaces for our intuition to flourish. This might involve mindfulness practices, digital detoxes, or simply spending quiet time in nature, allowing our intuitive insights to bubble to the surface.

Furthermore, as we continue to learn and adapt in the digital age, it's important to embrace a growth mindset – the belief that our abilities and intelligence can be developed over time. With a growth mindset, we see challenges not as insurmountable obstacles but as opportunities for learning and growth. We are more resilient in the face of setbacks and more willing to take risks, which are key to navigating the future.

Education will also play a significant role in fostering lifelong learning and adaptation. As we prepare for the future, we need to rethink our educational models. Traditional education, which often prioritizes rote memorization and standardized testing, may fall short in equipping individuals with the skills needed in the digital age. Instead, we need an educational system that promotes creativity, critical thinking, emotional intelligence, and intuitive skills – skills that are vital for lifelong learning and adaptation.

At a societal level, creating an environment that encourages lifelong learning and adaptation is equally important. This involves nurturing a culture that values continuous learning, curiosity, and innovation. It means creating opportunities for individuals to continually update their skills and knowledge, whether through ongoing education programs, online learning platforms, or community learning initiatives.

The path to the future may be uncharted and uncertain, but with lifelong learning and adaptation as our guiding principles, we can traverse it with confidence and resilience. By fostering our curiosity, resilience, intuition, and growth mindset, we can equip ourselves with the tools and perspective necessary to thrive in the digital age.

The journey of lifelong learning and adaptation is not a destination but a continuous process, an ongoing journey of discovery and growth. And as we embark on this journey, we are not just preparing for the future; we are actively shaping it. By committing to lifelong learning and adaptation, we are taking an active role in crafting a future that is not only technologically advanced but also deeply human and intuitive.

Ultimately, lifelong learning and adaptation in the digital age are not just about surviving but about thriving, about cultivating a rich and fulfilling life amidst rapid change and uncertainty. As we continue to learn, adapt, and grow, we also deepen our understanding of ourselves and the world around us, enriching our lives in profound and meaningful ways.

Future Predictions for the Role of Intuition in Society

As we gaze into the future, it is worth speculating how the role of intuition might evolve within society. While predictions in this space are inherently uncertain, understanding the likely trends can help us prepare for and shape the future. Let's consider how intuition might influence different areas of society.

One possible future is a world in which intuition plays an even greater role in decision-making than it does today. This is due in part to the increasing complexity of the world around us. With advancements in technology and an explosion of information, we're being asked to make sense of increasingly complex systems and phenomena. In this environment, our rational, analytical thinking – while still crucial – might not be enough.

Intuition, with its ability to synthesize complex information and draw upon a vast array of experiences and knowledge, could become an invaluable tool in navigating this complexity. From making business decisions to shaping public policies, from scientific research to artistic creation, intuition could become a fundamental component of our cognitive toolkit.

The burgeoning field of artificial intelligence (AI) provides a fascinating backdrop for the evolution of intuition. As AI systems become more sophisticated, they are being designed to mimic and even enhance human intuition. Algorithms that learn from vast amounts of data can spot patterns and make connections that might elude even the most intuitive human minds. Yet, it's crucial to recognize that these AI systems are not replacing human intuition, but augmenting it. AI can sift through mountains of data at a speed and scale beyond human capabilities, but it lacks the rich experiential context and emotional understanding that underpin human intuition.

In essence, the future might see a symbiotic relationship between AI and human intuition, where each complements the other. On the one hand, AI can provide the raw data and patterns; on the other hand, human intuition can provide the interpretive lens, infusing the data with meaning and significance based on our personal and collective experiences.

This rise of intuition in society will likely be accompanied by a corresponding rise in efforts to cultivate and hone our intuitive abilities. Intuition could be taught and nurtured in schools alongside traditional subjects, helping children to develop their intuitive skills from a young age. Businesses might invest in intuition training for their employees, recognizing that intuitive insights can lead to innovative solutions and effective decision-making. Meanwhile, individuals might seek out personal development practices that foster intuition, such as mindfulness, meditation, and reflective journaling.

As intuition becomes more recognized and valued, we might also see shifts in societal norms and attitudes. The dichotomy between rationality and intuition, long entrenched in Western thought, might give way to a more integrated view that sees both as essential facets of human cognition. There could be greater acceptance of intuitive decision-making in areas that have traditionally prized rationality, such as business, science, and government. Meanwhile, the cultural narrative that regards intuition as a mysterious, elusive phenomenon might evolve towards a view of intuition as a natural and developable human capacity.

In the realm of technology, we might see more digital tools and platforms designed to support and enhance intuition. These might include AI systems that help individuals tap into their intuition by providing pattern recognition and predictive capabilities, virtual reality experiences that stimulate intuitive insights, and social platforms that enable collective intuitive decision-making.

However, while there are many promising possibilities, it's also essential to acknowledge potential challenges. The increased role of intuition in society could lead to the devaluation of rational, evidence-based decision-making. There's a risk that intuition could be misused or exploited, with individuals or groups claiming intuitive insights as justification for unethical or harmful actions. Moreover, the marriage of AI and intuition could raise privacy concerns, as AI systems need access to personal data to provide intuitive predictions.

In navigating these challenges, a balanced approach will be key. Intuition and rationality are not opposing forces but complementary aspects of our cognition. While fostering our intuitive abilities, we also need to cultivate our critical thinking skills, ensuring that our intuitive insights are grounded in reality and subject to reasoned analysis. Similarly, while leveraging AI to augment our intuition, we need to implement robust ethical and privacy safeguards.

The future of intuition in society is indeed an exciting prospect. As we move forward, we have the opportunity to shape this future, to create a society where intuition is valued and nurtured, where it works in harmony with our rational minds, and where it serves to enhance our understanding, decision-making, and wellbeing. As we step into this future, we carry with us the wisdom of our intuitive selves, ready to navigate the complexities and possibilities of the digital age.

Chapter 10: The Sixth Sense and Digital Creativity

The Role of Intuition in Digital Art and Design

Digital art and design have transformed the creative landscape, ushering in new mediums, techniques, and possibilities. However, even as our creative tools become increasingly sophisticated, one fundamental aspect remains constant - the crucial role of intuition. While the tools may be digital, the artist's hand, guided by instinct, remains at the heart of the creative process.

Artists and designers have long relied on intuition. It fuels their imagination, guides their decision-making, and lends a distinctive voice to their creations. In the realm of digital art and design, the role of intuition takes on even more significance. Here, the canvas is boundless, the tools are infinite, and the possibilities are virtually limitless. In this expansive digital arena, intuition becomes the compass that points the way, steering the artist through the sea of options towards a vision that resonates with their inner truth.

Intuition helps to bridge the gap between the conscious and subconscious mind, enabling artists and designers to tap into deep-seated emotions, memories, and experiences that can imbue their work with depth and authenticity. By tuning into their intuition, they can access a wellspring of creativity that transcends the limitations of logical, linear thinking.

For digital artists, intuition can guide them in choosing the right tools, techniques, and aesthetic elements. It can inspire spontaneous decisions that add a touch of unpredictability and originality to their work. It can propel them to take risks, to break away from established norms, to venture into uncharted territories.

Similarly, for digital designers, intuition plays an indispensable role in shaping user experiences. While data and analytics provide valuable insights, it is often intuition that uncovers the most profound understandings of human behavior and emotion. Intuition allows designers to empathize with users, to intuit their needs, desires, and pain points, and to design solutions that speak to the human heart.

However, cultivating intuition in the digital realm isn't without its challenges. The very characteristics that make digital art and design so exciting - the myriad of tools, the infinite possibilities, the rapid pace of technological change - can also make it overwhelming. With so many options at our fingertips, it can be easy to lose sight of our intuitive voice amid the digital noise.

Overcoming this challenge requires a conscious effort to connect with our intuition amidst the digital whirlwind. It involves creating spaces of quiet and reflection, where we can tune out the external noise and tune into our inner voice. It entails nurturing our awareness, sensitivity, and receptivity - qualities that allow us to perceive and respond to our intuitive nudges.

Moreover, we can leverage digital tools to enhance our intuition. For instance, digital sketching tools can allow us to capture fleeting intuitive insights quickly. Virtual reality can immerse us in environments that stimulate our senses and evoke intuitive responses. AI systems can help us discover patterns and connections that might spark intuitive leaps.

The dynamic interplay between intuition and digital creativity holds exciting potential. As we move forward, we may witness an even more profound fusion of technology and intuition. We may see new forms of digital art and design that push the boundaries of what's possible, that embody the unique synthesis of human intuition and digital innovation.

It is a brave new world of creativity, where intuition, far from being overshadowed by technology, emerges as a guiding force, a beacon of light in the digital landscape. Whether you are an artist, a designer, or a lover of art, embracing your intuition can open the door to a vibrant world of digital creativity, a world where the human spirit and technological prowess dance in a mesmerizing duet.

Case Studies of Successful Digital Creators

In our exploration of the sixth sense and digital creativity, it's illuminating to study real-world examples. These individuals, often referred to as digital creators, have managed to tap into their intuition and wield digital tools to create remarkable works of art and design. Let's delve into the stories of a few such trailblazers and see what insights we can glean from their experiences.

Our first case study revolves around Sofia Liu, an avant-garde digital artist known for her surreal, dreamlike creations. Sofia's journey into digital art was borne out of a fascination with the interplay between reality and imagination. For Sofia, the digital canvas was a playground where she could give form to her intuitive insights and explore the boundaries of her creativity. Sofia's work is a testament to the power of intuition in guiding the creative process. Her art pieces, characterized by their ethereal quality and visual complexity, mirror the depth and nuance of her intuitive landscape. Sofia often speaks about the importance of quieting her mind and connecting with her inner self before she embarks on a piece. She likens it to tuning into a frequency, where her intuitive voice comes alive and guides her creative decisions.

Next, let's turn to Sam Johnson, a prominent figure in the world of digital design. Sam's intuition-led approach has led him to revolutionize user interface design, crafting digital experiences that are intuitive, engaging, and profoundly human. From his pioneering work in responsive design to his transformative contributions to accessibility, Sam has consistently demonstrated the power of intuition in understanding users and designing solutions that resonate with them on a deep, emotional level. He credits his success to his ability to empathize with users, to intuit their needs and desires, and to translate these insights into design decisions. His work exemplifies how intuition, when combined with data-driven insights, can elevate digital design to new heights.

We also have Yara Silva, an innovative digital creator who combines her passion for music and technology to create immersive audio-visual experiences. Yara's work straddles the line between art and technology, harnessing the power of digital tools to push the boundaries of music and visual storytelling. Her creations, often characterized by their intricate compositions and layered narratives, reflect her ability to tap into her intuition and synthesize diverse influences into a cohesive, compelling whole. Yara credits her intuitive sensibilities for her ability to capture the emotional essence of a piece and convey it through the interplay of sound and visuals.

Finally, we have Tan Wei, an AI artist who leverages artificial intelligence to create art that explores the human condition. Tan's work is a fascinating interplay of technology and intuition. He programs AI algorithms, feeds them with data, and then steps back, allowing his intuitive sense to guide him in selecting and refining the

AI's outputs. The resulting artworks, a symbiosis of machine learning and human intuition, challenge our notions of creativity and authorship.

These case studies offer compelling insights into how intuition and digital creativity can intertwine to create outstanding works of art and design. Each of these digital creators, in their unique ways, has managed to tap into their intuitive faculties, wield digital tools, and bring their visions to life in the digital realm. They remind us that, while our tools may be digital, the essence of creativity – that intuitive spark – remains profoundly human. By tuning into our intuition and embracing digital tools, we too can embark on our own journeys of digital creativity, unlocking new possibilities and enriching our creative lives.

Exercises to Stimulate Creative Intuition

One might question how to kindle the embers of creative intuition within. This unique, almost mystifying inner compass that seems to guide the pioneers of digital creativity. Can it be developed? The good news is, absolutely, yes. There are numerous exercises designed to stimulate and cultivate your creative intuition, serving as stepping stones in your own creative journey.

The first exercise is engaging in 'Free Writing'. Popularized by authors like Natalie Goldberg and Julia Cameron, free writing is an excellent method to bypass the logical mind and access the intuitive, creative self. It involves writing non-stop for a predetermined period, say 15-20 minutes, without worrying about grammar, punctuation, or even making sense. The primary rule is not to lift your pen off the paper and to allow whatever wants to emerge, to come forth. By doing this, you are, in essence, tuning in to your unconscious, the abode of intuition, and letting it communicate freely without the interruption of logical, linear thinking.

Second, consider 'Mind Mapping'. This technique, invented by Tony Buzan, encourages divergent thinking, an essential aspect of creativity. Start with a central concept and allow your mind to branch out into related ideas, writing each one down and linking them together. The result is a sprawling, organic map of thoughts, often revealing connections and insights that your logical mind might have missed. The aim is to let your intuition guide the flow of ideas, moving from one node to another, driven by instinct rather than linear reasoning.

Next is the practice of 'Meditation'. The essence of meditation is silence and presence, both of which are vital for intuition to thrive. By cultivating a practice of silence, you create space for your intuitive voice to be heard over the incessant chatter of the thinking mind. A simple meditation practice could be focusing on your breath for a few minutes each day. As your mind stills, you'll find your intuition becomes more prominent, providing creative insights that were drowned out by the noise of everyday thoughts.

'Visualization' serves as another effective exercise. It involves vividly picturing in your mind the outcome of a creative project or solution to a problem. By doing so, you engage the power of your subconscious mind and intuition, which can lead to creative breakthroughs and unexpected insights. Visualization is not just about 'seeing'; it involves all the senses. The more vividly you can engage your sensory perception in the visualization, the more effectively you can tap into your creative intuition.

Another useful tool is 'Dream Work'. Our dreams are a rich source of intuitive insights and creative ideas. The process of dream work involves recording your dreams and then reflecting upon them for potential insights and creative ideas. The act of translating the often-symbolic language of dreams into conscious understanding requires intuition and can, in turn, further develop it.

Lastly, the practice of 'Mindfulness' in your daily activities can also enhance your creative intuition. By being present and fully engaged in what you're doing, whether it's washing dishes, going for a walk, or painting a picture, you foster a state of open receptivity. This state is the breeding ground for intuition. When you're present, your mind is not cluttered with thoughts, worries, or plans, leaving it open for intuitive insights to arise.

Remember, these exercises are not one-size-fits-all. Everyone has their unique path to cultivating their creative intuition. The key lies in experimentation and persistence.

Try these techniques and see which ones resonate with you, which ones spark that intuitive ember within. Once you find what works, commit to it. Like any skill, developing your creative intuition takes practice. However, the rewards, as seen in the case studies of successful digital creators, are well worth the effort.

Who knows, maybe your name will be added to the list of those whose creative intuition has guided them to innovative and ground-breaking paths.

Chapter 11: The Sixth Sense, Intuition, and Digital Entrepreneurship

The Power of Intuition in Identifying Business Opportunities

Today, we live in a world where the line separating the digital and physical realms has become increasingly blurred. Consequently, the concept of entrepreneurship has evolved. At the confluence of this change, entrepreneurs often find themselves confronted with an overwhelming number of potential paths, each offering promising prospects. The pivotal question, then, is how to discern which path to pursue. It is within this labyrinth of possibilities that the sixth sense, intuition, emerges as a guiding light.

Intuition, often coined as a 'gut feeling' or 'inner voice,' is the ability to understand or know something immediately based on your instinctive feelings rather than conscious reasoning. Within the entrepreneurial landscape, intuition is instrumental in identifying business opportunities and making critical decisions.

The magic of intuition is its ability to pick up on patterns and connections that are not always visible to the conscious, analytical mind. It integrates vast amounts of information, pieces together complex patterns, and offers an immediate sense of direction. This function of intuition is especially valuable in the dynamic digital age, where data is abundant and changes occur at lightning speed.

The intuitive process is a form of rapid cognition that entrepreneur and author Malcolm Gladwell refers to as 'thin slicing' in his book, "Blink." He explains that we make sense of situations based on the thinnest slice of experience, a process that happens beneath our conscious awareness. In the entrepreneurial world, this ability to 'thin slice' can be the difference between seizing an opportunity and letting it pass by.

A classic example of intuition at play in the digital entrepreneurial sphere is that of Reed Hastings, the co-founder of Netflix. The idea for Netflix was born out of an intuition that people would prefer a more convenient, less restrictive way to rent movies. When Hastings was charged a hefty late fee for a movie rental, he sensed an opportunity for a different model - a flat-fee, unlimited rentals, without due dates, late fees, shipping, or handling fees. His intuitive insight gave birth to a business model that disrupted the traditional video rental industry and eventually morphed into a streaming giant.

While examples like Netflix illuminate the power of intuition in entrepreneurship, the process is far from being purely mystical or inaccessible. Much like any other skill, intuition can be nurtured and honed. It involves creating an environment conducive to hearing the soft whispers of your inner voice and developing the courage to trust its wisdom.

For digital entrepreneurs, this begins with carving out moments of silence amidst the constant digital noise. Regular periods of disconnection from the digital world, whether it's through meditation, walks in nature, or just sitting quietly, can help clear the mental clutter and amplify the voice of intuition. These quiet moments facilitate the movement from constant doing to simply being, a state in which intuitive insights are more likely to surface.

Cultivating a habit of introspection is another essential practice. Reflecting on one's experiences, thoughts, and feelings aids in developing self-awareness, a critical component of intuition. Keeping a journal, practicing mindfulness, or engaging in contemplative activities like yoga can facilitate this introspective journey.

One must also learn to heed the body's wisdom. Often, intuitive insights are accompanied by physical sensations - a gut feeling, a tingle, a sense of unease, or a feeling of excitement. By paying attention to these bodily signals and interpreting their messages, entrepreneurs can tap into their intuitive guidance system.

However, using intuition doesn't mean ignoring rational analysis. It's about achieving a balance between intuitive wisdom and logical reasoning, a synergy that author and psychologist Daniel Kahneman describes as 'thinking fast and slow.' This equilibrium is especially crucial in the digital realm, where data-driven decisions are the norm.

Finally, it's important to acknowledge that intuition is inherently linked with risk, as it might lead to paths that defy conventional wisdom. But as history shows, those who have dared to follow their intuition, like Steve Jobs or Elon Musk, have been the ones to disrupt industries and shape new paradigms. Their stories stand as a testament to the words of Albert Einstein: "The intuitive mind is a sacred gift and the rational mind is a faithful servant. We have created a society that honors the servant and has forgotten the gift."

As the digital age continues to evolve, the power of intuition in identifying and seizing business opportunities will only grow. By embracing this sixth sense, digital entrepreneurs can navigate the complex web of possibilities and chart a course that not only leads to success but also to novel solutions and creative innovations. They can become the trailblazers who guide us towards a future where digital technology is a seamless extension of human intuition. In the end, it's about heeding that inner call, trusting your instinct, and daring to leap into the unknown. After all, as French writer André Gide once said, "One does not discover new lands without consenting to lose sight of the shore for a very long time."

Case Studies: Entrepreneurs Who've Successfully Used Intuition

The world of entrepreneurship is fraught with uncertainty and brimming with potential. In this dynamic landscape, where analytical data and predictive algorithms are often hailed as the keys to success, there's a subtler, equally potent player at work - intuition. Intuition, that mysterious inner guidance system, has led many entrepreneurs to see what others could not, chart unknown territories, and transform nascent ideas into influential enterprises. This chapter will delve into some compelling case studies of successful entrepreneurs who've harnessed the power of their intuitive faculties.

Let's start with the legendary Steve Jobs, co-founder of Apple Inc. Jobs' intuition was arguably his most powerful tool, guiding him to revolutionize multiple industries, from personal computers and animated movies to music, phones, and tablet computing. A firm believer in the power of intuition, Jobs once said, "The people in the Indian countryside don't use their intellect like we do, they use their intuition instead... Intuition is a very powerful thing, more powerful than intellect, in my opinion. That's had a big impact on my work."

One critical decision driven by his intuition was the creation of the iPhone. Against market research that suggested a limited market for smartphones, Jobs sensed a shift in technology and consumer behavior. He followed his instinct and launched the iPhone, transforming the tech landscape forever. This decision wasn't based on hard data or calculated projections but stemmed from an inner conviction, a testament to the power of intuition in business.

Our next example takes us to the world of e-commerce with Jeff Bezos, founder of Amazon. Bezos left a high-paying job on Wall Street to start an online bookstore in the mid-90s, a decision that seemed irrational to many. But Bezos' intuition told him that the internet was about to change the world. He listened to his gut feeling, took the plunge, and launched Amazon out of his garage. Today, Amazon is a global powerhouse, revolutionizing the way we shop and reshaping the retail landscape.

Then there's Oprah Winfrey, a media mogul and philanthropist, whose success journey is deeply intertwined with her intuitive abilities. She trusts her gut feelings implicitly and credits intuition for much of her success. Oprah has often talked about the 'whispers' that guide her decisions, suggesting that paying attention to our feelings and hunches is a powerful way to navigate life and business. She once said, "I've trusted the still, small voice of intuition my entire life. And the only time I've made mistakes is when I didn't listen."

Sara Blakely, the founder of Spanx, also trusted her intuition in business decisions. She spent her savings on an idea that industry experts dismissed as destined to fail. Her gut feeling, however, told her that she was on to something.

Ignoring the naysayers, she persevered and turned Spanx into a billion-dollar company. Blakely believes intuition is like a muscle and becomes stronger with use. Her journey underscores the power of trusting one's instincts, even in the face of skepticism.

In the realm of digital entrepreneurship, we find the story of Brian Chesky and Joe Gebbia, co-founders of Airbnb. Their idea of creating a platform where people rent out their living space to strangers was initially met with disbelief. But Chesky and Gebbia, guided by their intuition, saw potential in creating a 'home away from home' experience for travelers. Their instinctive belief in the sharing economy's power, against all odds and criticisms, has resulted in one of the most successful startups of the digital age.

Lastly, there's the case of Elon Musk, a serial entrepreneur who's disrupted multiple industries, from online payments with PayPal to electric vehicles with Tesla and space travel with SpaceX. Musk's career is rife with examples of him trusting his intuition, making seemingly irrational decisions that later prove transformative. His vision of colonizing Mars, once considered a fanciful dream, now seems closer to reality, a testament to his intuitive foresight.

These cases underscore the role of intuition in entrepreneurial success. Each of these individuals listened to their inner voice, trusted their gut feelings, and took risks that others found unreasonable. Their stories highlight that intuition is not about ignoring data or rational analysis. It's about complementing these aspects with an internal guidance system, one that sees beyond the visible and tangible, often leading to innovation and breakthroughs.

However, it's crucial to note that harnessing intuition doesn't mean disregarding rational thought or due diligence. It's about creating a balance, a dance between the head and the heart. All these successful entrepreneurs are also known for their keen analytical abilities and tireless pursuit of knowledge, demonstrating that intuition and reason are not mutually exclusive but complementary forces. In the fast-paced, complex world of entrepreneurship, this symbiosis between intuition and rational thinking may well be the secret sauce for success.

The stories of these entrepreneurs offer powerful insights for anyone venturing into the entrepreneurial world. They underscore the importance of listening to your gut, daring to defy conventional wisdom, and having the courage to follow your instinct. This intuitive approach, when coupled with rational analysis and strategic planning, can open new vistas of opportunity, innovation, and success.

After all, entrepreneurship is as much about vision and instinct as it is about strategy and execution. It's about seeing what's invisible to others and daring to turn that vision into reality. These entrepreneurial journeys remind us that at the heart of every successful venture lies not just a great idea, but also the intuitive insight to see its potential and the courage to make it a reality.

Exercises for Cultivating Business Intuition

The journey of entrepreneurship, filled with uncertainties and endless decisions, can often feel like navigating an unfathomable maze. In such situations, having an intuitive compass can make all the difference. While we've looked at successful entrepreneurs who've leveraged their intuitive abilities, it's essential to understand that intuition is not an esoteric gift bestowed on a chosen few. It's a skill that can be nurtured and developed. This chapter aims to provide practical exercises for cultivating business intuition.

1. **Mindfulness Meditation**: At the root of intuition is a deep awareness of the present moment. Mindfulness meditation can help you achieve this by quietening the mind's noise and enhancing your awareness. Spend 10-15 minutes each day focusing on your breath or a particular sound. Whenever you notice your thoughts wandering, gently bring your attention back to your focus point. With regular practice, you'll notice an increased ability to tune into your intuitive signals.
2. **Sensory Observations**: An effective way to boost intuition is to enhance your sensory experiences. Spend a few minutes every day noticing things around you – the colors, the sounds, the textures,

the scents. Engaging your senses fully can help you become more receptive to the subtle intuitive cues that often get missed in the daily hustle.

3. **Intuition Journaling**: Keeping a dedicated journal to document your intuitive experiences can be invaluable. Record the hunches you get, the feelings that guide you, and the dreams that provide insight. Over time, you'll begin to see patterns, understand the language of your intuition, and gain confidence in your inner voice.
4. **Body Awareness Exercise**: Your body is an excellent intuitive ally, often providing physical signals (a gut feeling, a sudden chill, a sense of discomfort or excitement) that something is amiss or right. Spend a few minutes each day tuning into your body, noticing any sensations or tensions. Over time, you'll be able to better understand and trust your body's intuitive messages.
5. **Free Writing**: This exercise involves writing continuously for a set period without worrying about grammar or punctuation. It's about allowing your subconscious mind to express itself freely. You'll often find insights and intuitive nudges emerging through the words that flow unfiltered.
6. **The 'What If' Exercise**: When faced with a business decision, ask yourself, "What if I choose option A?" and then tune into your feelings. Do you feel a sense of peace, tension, excitement, or unease? Repeat the exercise with the other options. Your emotional response often provides intuitive clues about the right choice.

7. **Intuitive Listening**: In your interactions, practice listening with the intent to understand rather than respond. This not only helps in building stronger relationships but also hones your intuition as you'll learn to pick up on non-verbal cues, underlying emotions, and unsaid words.
8. **Nature Connection**: Spending time in nature can be profoundly healing and intuition-boosting. The natural world operates on instinct and intuition. Being in such an environment can help tune into your instinctive self.
9. **Dream Analysis**: Our subconscious mind often communicates through dreams. Keeping a dream journal and reflecting on the symbols and emotions in your dreams can provide intuitive insights.
10. **Practicing Patience**: Intuition operates in its own time, not always providing instant answers. Practice patience and allow the answers to emerge in their own time.

While these exercises can enhance your intuitive abilities, remember that intuition is like a friend who speaks when there's something important to say. It may not provide guidance on every mundane decision. But when it comes to significant choices, where the logical data is insufficient or ambiguous, your intuition can provide valuable insights that tip the scales in your favor.

Also, it's crucial to remember that intuition doesn't function in isolation. It works best in tandem with rational analysis. Use your analytical faculties to gather information, analyze, and understand the logical aspects. Then let your intuition weigh in to provide a more holistic perspective, helping you make decisions that align with your values, vision, and inner truth.

Cultivating intuition is not a one-time event but a lifelong journey of self-discovery and growth. With patience, practice, and openness, you can harness the power of intuition, enhancing not only your business decisions but also enriching your personal life. As you become more attuned to your intuition, you'll find it to be a reliable guide in the exciting entrepreneurial journey, helping you navigate the uncharted waters with a sense of confidence and inner peace. After all, as Albert Einstein once said, "The intuitive mind is a sacred gift and the rational mind is a faithful servant. We have created a society that honors the servant and has forgotten the gift."

It's time we honor and cultivate this precious gift.

Chapter 12: Intuition in Digital Education

The Role of Intuition in Online Learning

As we journey further into the digital age, education continues to transform, with online learning becoming an integral part of the education landscape. Distance learning platforms, Massive Open Online Courses (MOOCs), and even traditional schools and universities have incorporated online components into their curricula, expanding access to education worldwide. Yet, amidst this sweeping digital transition, the role of intuition in online learning remains a crucial yet often under-explored topic.

Intuition, as we've been exploring throughout this book, is our subconscious mind's way of rapidly processing information and making decisions. It's the flash of insight that guides us when rational analysis falls short or the instinctive understanding that emerges without deliberate thought. In an online learning environment, this intuitive knowing can play a critical role in facilitating an enriching and productive educational experience.

Online learning poses unique challenges that are different from those in traditional classrooms. The digital realm can feel isolated and impersonal, and the absence of physical cues can make communication more challenging. Furthermore, learners often have to self-direct their study, manage their time efficiently, and troubleshoot technological issues – all while grappling with the cognitive demands of learning new material.

In navigating these challenges, intuition can be a powerful ally. When a learner taps into their intuitive knowledge, they can better discern which resources to focus on, when to seek help, how to approach their studies, and even how to interact effectively in digital spaces. Intuition can guide learners in choosing the right courses, recognizing when they've understood a concept, and knowing when to pause for better assimilation of knowledge.

Intuition's role extends to educators as well. Instructors who are intuitively in sync with their students can create engaging online learning experiences. They can discern what might be hindering a student's progress or sense when to introduce new concepts. Intuition can guide them in designing curriculum, moderating discussions, providing feedback, and fostering a supportive and inclusive online learning environment.

Integrating intuition into the digital education landscape begins with acknowledging its value. Both educators and learners must understand that logic and intuition are not conflicting entities but complementary facets of the human cognitive experience. Encouraging intuition's use in online learning is about creating a space where the logical and the intuitive can coexist, enhancing the learning experience.

Practically, this might look like educators encouraging students to trust their gut feelings when tackling complex problems or to follow their curiosity in exploring additional resources. It might involve integrating reflective practices into the curriculum to help students tune in to their intuitive understanding. For educators, it might mean trusting their hunches about how to facilitate an online discussion or intuitively adapting their teaching style to better suit the digital platform.

But how does one cultivate intuition in the context of digital education? There is no one-size-fits-all answer, as the intuitive process is highly individual. However, it often involves quietening the noise of the outside world to tune into the inner self. This might mean taking a few moments of silence before starting an online class or incorporating mindfulness practices into the daily routine. It also involves staying open and receptive, trusting the intuitive process, and recognizing that it's okay not to have all the answers immediately.

In a world increasingly dominated by data and analysis, intuition can feel like a soft whisper amidst a cacophony of voices. But as we've seen throughout this book, intuition has the potential to guide us in profound and meaningful ways. In the realm of digital education, it can enhance the learning experience, foster deeper connections, and ultimately, contribute to building a more inclusive, accessible, and effective educational landscape in the digital age.

So, as we continue to navigate this digital education landscape, let us remember that our sixth sense – our intuition – is as valuable a tool in our learning toolkit as any. Whether we're educators designing online courses or learners trying to master a new subject, our intuition can guide us, enrich our experiences, and illuminate our paths in ways we might not fully comprehend but can certainly appreciate and value. Embrace your intuitive knowledge, trust its wisdom, and see how it transforms your digital education journey.

Developing a Sixth Sense for Effective Learning Strategies

The world of digital education can be a maze of information and decisions. From selecting the appropriate courses to determining the best method to absorb and process new concepts, students and educators alike can feel overwhelmed. How can we navigate this vast expanse of options and create an effective learning experience? As we've explored throughout this book, the answer may lie in harnessing the power of intuition – our 'sixth sense'.

Intuition, the immediate understanding that we often experience without the conscious use of reasoning, is a crucial resource that can guide us towards more effective learning strategies. It acts like an internal compass, pointing us towards what resonates with us and away from what does not. Let's delve deeper into how we can cultivate this intuitive sense to enhance our learning experience in the digital landscape.

1. Trusting the Learning Process

Firstly, developing a sixth sense for learning involves trust – trust in the process, trust in the natural curiosity that fuels our learning, and trust in ourselves. Sometimes, an online course might not click immediately, or a particular concept may seem daunting. Intuition helps us trust that with time and effort, understanding will follow.

How do you cultivate this trust? Begin by acknowledging that it's okay not to know everything right away. Learning is a process, and sometimes that process involves wrestling with uncertainty before clarity emerges. Encourage yourself to stay patient and open-minded, and observe how this trust enhances your learning experience.

2. Following Your Interests

Intuition can serve as a guide to discovering what truly interests us. Often, our gut feelings can tell us what topics spark our curiosity and what areas might feel more tedious. This intuitive knowing can be crucial in the vast landscape of digital education, where the sheer variety of options can be overwhelming.

To harness this aspect of intuition, regularly check in with your feelings as you navigate different subjects. Pay attention to what ignites a spark of interest, and don't be afraid to delve deeper into these areas. This intuitive approach can lead you towards a more enjoyable and fulfilling learning journey.

3. Sensing Understanding

Often, our intuition can signal when we've truly understood a concept. You might have experienced those 'Aha!' moments when a difficult idea suddenly becomes clear. This is intuition at play, bridging the gap between conscious effort and subconscious understanding.

To tune into this aspect of intuition, be attentive to these moments of clarity. Recognize them as milestones in your learning journey. Over time, you'll get better at sensing when such an intuitive understanding has occurred, allowing you to move forward confidently.

4. Intuitive Time Management

In online learning, managing time effectively can be a significant challenge. Here too, intuition can lend a helping hand. Your intuitive sense can guide you in deciding when to take breaks for better assimilation of knowledge, or when to push through and finish a module.

To develop this skill, start by listening to your body and mind's signals. If you notice your concentration waning, it might be a cue from your intuition that it's time for a short break. On the other hand, if you feel energized and focused, it might be an indication to seize the momentum and continue learning.

5. Recognizing the Need for Help

Finally, intuition can be instrumental in acknowledging when we need assistance. It can be easy to get stuck in the cycle of trying to figure everything out on our own, especially in an online learning setting where we might be physically alone. However, intuition can help us recognize

when it's time to reach out for help – whether from a teacher, a peer, or through additional resources.
To harness this intuitive understanding, be honest with yourself about your struggles and uncertainties. If you intuitively feel that you're not grasping a concept, take it as a cue to seek assistance. Remember, asking for help is not a sign of weakness but a step towards growth and understanding.

Cultivating a sixth sense for effective learning strategies is not about discarding logical thinking. Instead, it involves creating a synergy between intuition and logic, combining the power of both to enhance your learning experience.

As you navigate the landscape of digital education, remember that your intuition is a resource ready to be tapped. Embrace it as you would a trusted guide. Trust its wisdom, follow its guidance, and allow it to lead you on a path of enriching and effective learning. The journey towards harnessing your sixth sense in learning is a voyage of self-discovery, offering insights not just into your academic interests but into your personal strengths and potentials as well. Embrace this journey with an open mind, and witness how it transforms your learning experience.

Case Studies: Successful Learning Outcomes Through Intuition

While the theory of intuition and its role in learning can be an engaging subject, it becomes even more compelling when we can see its real-life application. In this section, we will explore a few case studies that illustrate the successful use of intuition in digital learning environments. Each story showcases unique individuals who embraced their intuitive senses to navigate the complex landscape of digital education, resulting in beneficial learning outcomes.

Please note, as the following people are not public figures, their surnames have been withheld so as to protect their privacy.

The Story of Lily: Trusting the Learning Process

Lily was an adult learner who decided to take up a digital course on graphic design. Despite having no prior experience or education in the field, she was guided by a strong gut feeling that this was the right path for her. During the first few weeks, Lily struggled to grasp the various tools and concepts. The unfamiliar terminologies and intricate software often left her overwhelmed.

But Lily chose to trust her intuition. She recognized that the early struggles were a part of her learning journey. Instead of giving up, she persisted and began to see slow but steady improvement. Her designs started taking shape, and she was able to implement the techniques learned in the course effectively.

Lily's story demonstrates how intuition can foster trust in the learning process. Even when the material was challenging, she listened to her internal compass, which guided her to persevere. By doing so, she was able to overcome initial hurdles and achieve her learning goals.

The Story of Noah: Following His Interests

Noah was a college student enrolled in an online computer science degree program. Early in his studies, he discovered a multitude of courses, ranging from data structures to web development. Overwhelmed by the choices, he was unsure which direction to take.

He started exploring different courses but found himself particularly drawn towards cybersecurity. Every time he engaged with content related to this subject, he felt an unmistakable pull. Even though his academic advisor suggested a more traditional path like software engineering, Noah decided to trust his intuition and specialize in cybersecurity.

This intuitive decision led him to excel in his studies. His genuine interest in the subject made learning enjoyable, and he was able to grasp complex concepts easily. His final project on 'Emerging Threats in Cybersecurity' received high recognition, leading to an internship opportunity at a leading tech company.

The Story of Mia: Sensing Understanding

Mia was an experienced professional undertaking an online MBA to further her career. During her strategic management course, she was introduced to the BCG Matrix – a strategic tool for portfolio management. Despite numerous attempts, she struggled to understand the concept.

One day, while reviewing the material again, she had an 'Aha!' moment. All the components of the BCG Matrix suddenly fell into place. She intuitively understood the relationship between market growth, market share, and how businesses could use this matrix to make strategic decisions.

This intuitive understanding was reflected in her assignments, where she applied the BCG Matrix to various business scenarios effectively. Her professors and peers acknowledged her deep understanding, showcasing that her intuitive moment of learning had led to practical, successful outcomes.

The Story of Max: Intuitive Time Management

Max was a high school student who was juggling school work, part-time employment, and an online course in creative writing. Given his busy schedule, efficient time management was critical.

Max found that he was most productive early in the mornings. Even though conventional advice suggested studying in the afternoon, Max chose to follow his intuitive understanding of his body's rhythm. He dedicated his early morning hours to the online course when his mind was fresh and alert.

This intuitive time management led to a fruitful learning experience. Max was able to engage with the course content effectively and even produced several well-received pieces of writing. Despite a busy schedule, he successfully completed the course and enriched his writing skills.

These case studies highlight the role intuition can play in facilitating successful learning outcomes. Whether it's trusting the process like Lily, following genuine interests like Noah, sensing understanding like Mia, or managing time effectively like Max, intuition proves to be a guiding force. Each of these learners tuned into their inner compass, leading them to a rewarding and effective educational journey in the digital world. Their stories serve as a testament to the power of intuition in learning, and an inspiration for us all to listen more closely to our own intuitive senses.

Chapter 13: Ethical Considerations in the Digital Age

Ethical Use of Digital Intuition and the Sixth Sense

As the exploration of intuition and the sixth sense in the digital world expands, so too does the necessity to address ethical considerations that come with it. We live in an era where data is often termed as 'the new oil', and personal information is the currency of choice for many digital platforms. The amalgamation of intuition, extra-sensory perception (ESP), and digital technology opens up a Pandora's box of ethical dilemmas that must be carefully evaluated and mitigated.

When we talk about digital intuition, we're referring to the application of intuition and ESP in digital spaces. This might include intuitive choices made in digital learning, as we've seen in previous chapters, or it could be more complex manifestations such as the use of intuitive AI and data-driven predictions. While these applications can certainly be beneficial, they also bring forth a series of ethical questions around privacy, consent, accuracy, and responsibility.

Privacy is one of the most pertinent ethical issues in the digital age. When we apply intuition and ESP digitally, it often involves the collection and analysis of personal data. For instance, AI systems that 'intuitively' recommend products or services are typically based on algorithms that analyze a user's online behavior. This raises questions: how much of this personal data collection is acceptable? What is the line between a helpful suggestion and a breach of privacy?

Ethical usage of digital intuition must uphold the principles of data minimization and purpose limitation. Data minimization refers to the practice of only collecting the data necessary for a particular purpose, while purpose limitation involves using the collected data solely for the reason it was collected. These principles are cornerstones of responsible data handling and can help prevent misuse of personal information.

Alongside privacy, consent is another critical ethical concern. Users must be informed about how their data is being collected, analyzed, and utilized. They should also have the right to opt-out of such data collection or to request the removal of their data. The concept of 'informed consent' should be a fundamental practice in any digital platform utilizing intuition and ESP.

Accuracy is another point of contention when it comes to the ethical use of digital intuition. When digital platforms make predictions or recommendations based on a user's data, there's an implicit assumption that these insights are accurate. However, this isn't always the case. Algorithms can and do make mistakes. Therefore, it's ethically important to recognize the fallibility of digital intuition and provide avenues for correcting any inaccuracies that might arise.

Lastly, the notion of responsibility is integral to ethical considerations in digital intuition and ESP. Who holds the responsibility when things go wrong? If an AI makes an inaccurate prediction, who is held accountable? When businesses use intuition to make decisions, they must also be prepared to accept responsibility for the outcomes of these decisions.

These ethical considerations highlight the complexity of intertwining intuition, ESP, and digital technology. They emphasize the need for establishing ethical guidelines and safeguards to ensure that these advanced capabilities are used responsibly and respectfully. The balance of leveraging these abilities while upholding ethical principles is a delicate task that needs ongoing dialogue and adaptation. As we continue to explore the potential of the sixth sense in the digital age, let us do so with a firm commitment to uphold the ethical principles that maintain our respect for individual rights and privacy.

Privacy and Consent in the Age of Data Overload

Our current era, characterized by the ubiquity of digital technology, could be aptly described as an "age of data overload." With every click, scroll, or interaction online, massive amounts of data are generated, collected, and analyzed. The intersection of this data abundance and digital intuition brings a heightened urgency to address privacy and consent, two fundamental principles of ethical data handling.

In our digitally interconnected world, the concept of privacy has dramatically evolved. Privacy is no longer solely about seclusion or keeping our personal lives hidden from public view. Instead, in the digital realm, privacy revolves around our personal data: who has access to it, how it's used, and the controls we have over it. Personal data acts as digital breadcrumbs, narrating detailed stories about our preferences, behaviors, and identities. When intuition and extra-sensory perception are applied to this data, the narratives become more profound, adding another layer of sensitivity to this personal information.

Given the intimacy of these digital narratives, privacy stands at the forefront of ethical considerations. Not all users are comfortable with their personal data being collected and analyzed, particularly when it's used to draw intuitive insights about their behaviors and preferences. Privacy in this context becomes about the ability to control our digital identities and narratives. It's about ensuring that we have the right to shape and restrict how our personal information is accessed and used.

Navigating privacy in the age of data overload involves being proactive about the data we generate. It's about understanding the digital trails we leave behind and recognizing their potential uses and misuses. Digital literacy, therefore, becomes crucial, equipping users with the knowledge to navigate privacy settings, understand data policies, and make informed choices about their data.

While privacy is about control over personal data, consent is about the choice. It's about ensuring that users have the right to decide if, how, and when their data is collected and used. In the context of digital intuition, informed consent becomes a crucial ethical principle. It’s about ensuring that users are aware that their data will not only be collected but may also be used to derive intuitive insights.

Informed consent is an ongoing process, not a one-time agreement. It requires clear, straightforward communication from digital platforms about how user data will be used and the implications of these uses. Users should also have the right to withdraw their consent at any time and request the removal or anonymization of their data.

Despite these principles of privacy and consent, challenges persist. The language in privacy policies can often be dense and legalistic, making it hard for users to understand what they're consenting to. There's also the question of power dynamics. Given the necessity of certain digital platforms, can users genuinely make a free choice to withhold their data without experiencing disadvantages?

Addressing these challenges requires a multi-faceted approach. Policymakers must push for clearer, user-friendly privacy policies and stronger regulations around data use. Digital platforms, on the other hand, must be committed to transparency and respect for user privacy, making efforts to democratize the power over data.

Educators and institutions also have a role to play in promoting digital literacy, enabling individuals to understand the implications of their digital footprints. By being informed about their data trails and the principles of privacy and consent, individuals can better navigate the digital world, safeguarding their digital identities and narratives.

In the end, the quest to uphold privacy and consent in the age of data overload is a collective responsibility. It's a shared journey among users, digital platforms, and policymakers. As we delve deeper into the possibilities of intuition and extra-sensory perception in the digital world, let's also ensure we're championing the principles of privacy and consent, ensuring that the data overload doesn't overshadow our right to control our digital identities and narratives.

Navigating the Moral Landscape of Digital Intuition

As we plunge deeper into the digital age, we find ourselves at the crossroads of technological advancement and ethical implications. One such area is the realm of digital intuition, where data, machine learning, and intuitive insights intertwine, creating a complex moral landscape that needs careful navigation.

At the heart of digital intuition lies the concept of understanding and predicting human behavior through data. It's about using sophisticated algorithms to uncover patterns, trends, and predictions that might not be immediately visible. With this, a host of ethical considerations arises, dealing with issues such as consent, privacy, fairness, and accountability.

When we talk about digital intuition, we're fundamentally talking about humanizing data. It involves collecting, analyzing, and interpreting data in a way that reveals not just our actions but our intentions, thoughts, and potential future behaviors. As a result, it raises questions about what data should be collected, how it should be used, and who should have access to it.

Consent is the cornerstone of this moral landscape. As digital intuition typically involves analyzing personal data to derive insights, it is vital that individuals provide informed consent. However, there's a challenge of ensuring this consent is indeed 'informed.' Do individuals fully understand the potential implications of their data being used for intuitive insights? Are they aware of how these insights could be utilized? Informed consent isn't just about saying 'yes' to data collection; it's about understanding the why and how of data use.

Closely related to consent is the principle of privacy. Privacy in the digital age isn't just about what's kept secret; it's about having control over our personal data. In the realm of digital intuition, this privacy extends to our digital narratives – the stories our data tells about us. It's about ensuring that individuals have the ability to control these narratives, including who gets to read them and how they are interpreted.

A significant concern in this moral landscape is data bias. As digital intuition relies on algorithms trained on vast datasets, there's a risk of reinforcing biases present in the data. If the data reflects societal prejudices, the intuitive insights derived could potentially perpetuate these biases, leading to unfair outcomes. Therefore, it's crucial to ensure the fairness of digital intuition, actively working to identify and mitigate any biases in the data.

Lastly, there's the issue of accountability. With digital intuition largely powered by complex algorithms, it can be challenging to understand how specific insights are derived. This opacity can lead to a lack of accountability, where it's unclear who's responsible if things go wrong. Navigating the moral landscape of digital intuition requires clear accountability structures, ensuring that there's always someone answerable for the actions and outcomes of these systems.

So, how do we navigate this moral landscape? First, we need to embrace transparency. Businesses, researchers, and data analysts using digital intuition should be upfront about their methods, the data they use, and the potential implications of their work. They should ensure that individuals are fully informed and able to provide meaningful consent.

Second, we need to advocate for privacy by design. This approach involves building privacy protections into the very fabric of data systems, from the ground up. It means not just respecting privacy but actively working to protect it, giving individuals more control over their personal data and digital narratives.

Third, we need to combat data bias. This involves actively seeking out and addressing biases in the data, ensuring that digital intuition leads to fair and unbiased insights. It requires constant vigilance, ongoing evaluation, and a commitment to improving data practices.

Lastly, we must insist on accountability. This requires clear lines of responsibility for the actions and outcomes of digital intuition systems. It involves setting up robust oversight mechanisms, including third-party audits and regulations, to ensure accountability.

Navigating the moral landscape of digital intuition isn't easy. It requires a fine balance of advancing technological capabilities while safeguarding ethical principles.

However, it's a journey we must embark on, ensuring that the digital age's potential is harnessed responsibly and ethically. By advocating for transparency, privacy, fairness, and accountability, we can navigate this complex landscape, ensuring that digital intuition serves us all, not just a select few.

Chapter 14: Conclusion - Embracing the Future of Intuition

The Evolving Nature of Intuition and the Sixth Sense

As we wind our way towards the final stages of our journey into understanding intuition and the sixth sense in this digital era, it's important to reflect upon the evolving nature of these unique human capabilities and what they hold for our future. Through this exploration, we have analyzed the multiple facets of intuition, touched upon its scientific, psychological, and even metaphysical aspects, and delved into how the digital age is reshaping our understanding and utilization of our sixth sense.

At the heart of our investigation, we found that intuition remains an elusive yet essential aspect of the human cognitive apparatus. It serves as a guide, a mentor whispering wisdom that's not always consciously processed but holds immense significance in our decision-making processes. The sixth sense, often perceived as the realm of the mystical, is nothing more than our brain's way of cutting corners, jumping to conclusions without engaging in exhaustive analytical processing.

In the digital age, the nature of intuition is evolving. It's being affected, refined, and even amplified by the proliferation of technology and data. With AI and machine learning, we have tools that can mimic and even enhance human intuition, sifting through vast amounts of information to make predictions and judgements, often more accurately and quickly than humans can.

However, the advent of such digital intuition also presents challenges and raises ethical considerations, as we've explored in preceding chapters. Balancing the utility of intuitive digital systems with the principles of privacy, consent, and fairness is a nuanced task, one that we are collectively learning to navigate.

Looking ahead, we're on the brink of an era where intuition, the sixth sense, and technology are so interwoven that it will be hard to tell where one ends and the other begins. Our intuitive capabilities, coupled with the power of digital tools, hold the potential to reshape our world, influencing fields as diverse as education, business, healthcare, and beyond.

In the realm of education, digital intuition could revolutionize learning, making it more personalized and effective. In business, it can drive decision-making, allowing leaders to navigate uncertainty with greater confidence. In healthcare, it could lead to more accurate diagnoses and treatments, significantly improving patient outcomes.

Yet, with great power comes great responsibility. As we leverage our sixth sense and integrate it with technology, we need to be mindful of ethical considerations. Transparency, accountability, and the protection of personal data should remain at the forefront of our actions. Ensuring informed consent, combating data bias, and advocating for privacy by design are vital to preserving trust in this rapidly advancing field.

Moreover, we must remember that while digital tools can enhance our intuition, they cannot replace the human touch. Our intuition is more than just patterns and predictions; it's informed by our experiences, emotions, and values. It's an inherently human capacity, one that gives us the ability to empathize, innovate, and connect with others on a profound level.

As we stride into this new era, we should view the evolving nature of intuition and the sixth sense not with trepidation but with a sense of excitement and anticipation. We're standing at the cusp of a frontier that holds infinite possibilities for human cognitive capabilities. Embracing this future requires an open mind, a respect for ethics, and a deep understanding of the immense value that our intuitive capabilities bring to our lives.

Ultimately, the future of intuition in the digital age is one of collaboration – a symbiosis between our natural intuitive abilities and the power of digital technology. It's a future that promises to be as exciting as it is challenging, filled with opportunities to unlock the full potential of the human mind. As we move forward, let's do so with an appreciation for the intricate beauty of our intuition and a commitment to harnessing its power responsibly and ethically in our ever-evolving digital world.

Final Reflections: Embracing Uncertainty and Trusting Your Intuition

The journey we have embarked on together throughout the pages of this book has allowed us to delve deep into the mysterious yet fascinating world of intuition and the sixth sense. This exploration has not been a path along a linear and predictable landscape, but a winding road filled with intriguing discoveries, bold propositions, and challenging questions. However, a critical element that consistently emerges from our voyage is the potential and power of trusting our intuition, particularly as we navigate an era marked by increasing digitalization and a high degree of uncertainty.

The digital age, with all its complexities and paradoxes, has introduced unprecedented levels of uncertainty in our lives. The constant influx of information, the rapid pace of technological innovation, and the blur between virtual and physical realities all contribute to an environment where change is the only constant. Yet, amidst this flux and instability, the power of our intuition, our innate sixth sense, remains a steadfast ally, guiding us towards decisions and actions that align with our deepest values and authentic selves.

Uncertainty, although often perceived as unsettling, is not necessarily a foe to be vanquished. Instead, it can be embraced as a catalyst for growth and transformation. The uncertainty inherent in our digital era can spur us to tap into our intuitive abilities more effectively and purposefully. Rather than resisting change and unpredictability, we can view them as opportunities to hone our intuition, helping us navigate the ambiguous terrains of life with more resilience and optimism.

One might ask, how does one begin to trust intuition amidst a sea of uncertainty? The answer lies in understanding and accepting intuition as an integral part of our cognitive machinery. It's not a mystical, inexplicable force, but a natural, inherent capability honed through years of experience and learning. Intuition is our subconscious mind connecting the dots, drawing on stored patterns and insights to provide us with quick, often accurate judgments.

Cultivating trust in our intuition requires acknowledging and valuing its role in our decision-making processes. It involves consciously tapping into our gut feelings, not dismissing them as baseless or irrational, but considering them as vital pieces of information. Intuition, when used in conjunction with rational analysis, can enhance our decision-making ability, offering a more holistic view of situations and challenges.

Moreover, trusting our intuition requires practice. It's akin to a muscle that strengthens with use. As we make small decisions based on intuition and observe the outcomes, we gradually build confidence in our intuitive abilities. This process, however, requires patience and a willingness to make mistakes. We must remember that intuition, although powerful, is not infallible. It's a guide, not a guarantee.

Embracing uncertainty in our digital era also involves being comfortable with not knowing. It necessitates letting go of the need for absolute control and predictability. The digital age, with its inherent unpredictability, can serve as a training ground for developing this comfort with ambiguity. It can push us to rely on our intuition, allowing us to discover its strength and value.

Further, as we tread the path of intuition in the digital age, we must also be cognizant of ethical and moral considerations. In a world where digital technology can mimic and even enhance intuition, navigating the balance between utility and ethics becomes vital. Transparency, accountability, and the safeguarding of personal data must be integral parts of our journey towards leveraging digital intuition.

As we move forward, embracing uncertainty and trusting our intuition can help us unlock our full potential. By harnessing the power of our sixth sense in the digital age, we can navigate the tumultuous waves of change with grace and confidence. We can foster personal growth, catalyze innovation, and contribute meaningfully to our communities and societies.

Indeed, intuition can serve as our inner compass, guiding us through the dynamic, complex landscapes of our personal and professional lives. It is an ally waiting to be recognized, a silent whisper nudging us towards our authentic selves. By honoring our intuition, we acknowledge the wisdom within us, empowering ourselves to navigate the future, no matter how uncertain, with a sense of confidence and inner peace.

Ultimately, our journey through the realm of intuition and the sixth sense in the digital age is an invitation to each one of us. It invites us to venture beyond the familiar shores of logic and rationality, to delve into the rich, often untapped reservoir of intuition within us. It encourages us to embrace uncertainty as a companion rather than an adversary, transforming it into a canvas for growth, discovery, and transformation.

As we continue to navigate the complex contours of our digital era, let's do so with an open heart and a curious mind, trusting in the power of our intuition, and embracing the exciting possibilities that uncertainty brings. Remember, in this rapidly changing world, our intuition, our sixth sense, can be our most reliable guide, helping us chart a course towards a future that reflects our deepest aspirations and dreams.

Additional Resources for Enhancing Your Digital Intuition

Books, Online Courses, and Communities

In the quest to develop and refine our sixth sense in the digital age, a multifaceted approach often yields the most significant results. While personal experience is a valuable teacher, further resources such as books, online courses, and active communities can provide additional insights, skills, and knowledge that facilitate our understanding and application of digital intuition. These resources offer an expansive range of perspectives and methodologies that cater to diverse learning styles and personal preferences.

Books

1. "Blink: The Power of Thinking Without Thinking" by Malcolm Gladwell: This book delves into the process and impact of intuitive thinking and snap judgements.
2. "The Power of Intuition" by Gary Klein: Klein's book offers an in-depth exploration of intuition, enriched with practical techniques for enhancing intuitive abilities.
3. "The Field" by Lynne McTaggart: The author investigates the science behind intuition and how

an understanding of quantum physics can boost your intuitive senses.

Online Courses

1. "Developing Your Intuition for Business Success" on Coursera: This course offers practical tools to incorporate intuition in business decision-making.
2. "Improving Your Intuition" on Udemy: A course dedicated to strengthening intuition through exercises and practice.
3. "Mindfulness and Meditation" courses on Khan Academy: These courses can help enhance intuitive abilities by encouraging a stronger connection with the inner self.

Communities

1. Reddit communities like r/IntuitiveDominant: An online platform for people to share their experiences and seek advice on intuition.
2. The "Intuition Development" group on Facebook: A group dedicated to fostering discussions and providing resources about intuition.
3. Meetup groups such as "Intuition, Feelings, and Fun!" : These offer in-person meetings and activities designed to nurture intuition.

Practical Exercises for Developing Your Digital Sixth Sense

Exercises for Daily Practice

Building a stronger digital sixth sense is like any other skill—it requires daily practice and consistent dedication. Here are some exercises that can help you build your intuitive abilities in the digital age.

1. Mindful Media Consumption
The first step in developing your digital sixth sense is to be mindful of your media consumption. Pay close attention to the emotions, thoughts, and physical sensations that arise when you engage with digital content. Does a particular article make you uneasy? Do certain social media posts evoke strong emotions? Take note of these intuitive responses, and with time, you'll begin to discern patterns that inform your digital intuition.

2. Digital Detox
Take time each day to disconnect from digital devices. This could be a few hours in the morning, or perhaps in the evening. The purpose is to provide space for your mind to process the digital information it's absorbed. Just as sleep

helps our brains consolidate learning, taking a digital break helps integrate your digital experiences into your intuition.

3. Online Empathy Practice

Use digital communication as a playground for empathy. When you read comments or posts online, try to intuit the emotional state of the person behind the words. Consider their perspective, their possible motivations. This not only enhances your empathetic skills but also nurtures your intuitive understanding of people's digital expressions.

4. Intuitive Web Navigation

Let your intuition guide your online exploration. Start by opening your web browser. Without a specific destination in mind, allow your intuition to guide your clicks. Be observant of where you end up. You might be surprised by what your intuition leads you to discover.

5. Reflective Journaling

Keep a digital intuition journal. Document your online experiences, noting how your intuition guided you. Did you have a hunch about a piece of information that turned out to be important? Did a gut feeling steer you away from a digital interaction that later proved to be problematic? By documenting these instances, you reinforce your intuitive skills and teach your subconscious mind to value this sixth digital sense.

6. Mindful Alerts
Establish mindful alerts throughout the day using digital reminders. Every time the reminder goes off, check in with yourself. How are you feeling? What's on your mind? This consistent self-check can boost your self-awareness, a critical component in honing intuition.

The path to developing your digital sixth sense is personal and unique. Not every exercise will resonate with everyone, and that's okay. The key is to find practices that work for you and align with your lifestyle. Commit to these exercises, and with time, you'll see your digital intuition flourish.

Customizing Your Practice to Your Digital Habits

Customizing Your Practice to Your Digital Habits

Every individual's relationship with the digital world is unique. From our choices of platforms to the frequency of our online interactions, we all engage with the digital landscape differently. Consequently, developing your digital sixth sense is not a one-size-fits-all proposition. Here's how you can customize your intuitive practices to align with your digital habits.

1. Identifying Your Digital Landscape
Start by taking inventory of your online behaviors. How much time do you spend online? Which platforms do you

visit most often? What kind of content do you consume? Once you have a clear understanding of your digital landscape, you can design practices that are relevant to your online interactions.

2. Timing Your Practices

If you are an avid morning email checker, consider scheduling your mindful media consumption practice after this routine. If you find yourself mindlessly scrolling through social media in the afternoon, that might be a good time for a digital detox. Align your practices with your habits to enhance their effectiveness.

3. Choosing Relevant Exercises

Not all exercises will resonate with every individual. For instance, if your online interactions are mostly work-related, the empathy practice might not be as relevant for you. On the other hand, if you engage in frequent online discussions, this could be a valuable exercise. Choose practices that make sense for your digital habits.

4. Establishing Realistic Goals

If you're online for the majority of your day, it might not be feasible to take several hours of digital detox. However, you could start with short breaks, gradually increasing your offline time. Set realistic goals for your practices that reflect your lifestyle.

5. Adapting and Evolving Your Practices

Your digital habits will change with time, and your intuitive practices should evolve too. Regularly reassess your digital landscape and adjust your practices accordingly. Stay flexible and open to change.

6. Making Use of Digital Tools

Leverage digital tools to support your practices. Use app timers to remind you to take a digital detox, or journal apps to document your intuitive experiences. These tools can make your practices more accessible and convenient.

Developing your digital sixth sense is a journey of self-discovery. It requires patience, dedication, and a willingness to adapt. By customizing your practices to your digital habits, you're taking a crucial step towards unlocking your intuition in the digital age.

Frequently Asked Questions

1. What is digital intuition? Digital intuition refers to the application of intuitive thinking in our engagement with the digital world. It involves utilizing our innate ability to understand or know something without conscious reasoning while interacting with digital devices, platforms, or ecosystems.

2. Is digital intuition the same as extra-sensory perception? Not necessarily. While extra-sensory perception also pertains to obtaining information beyond the usual sensory channels, digital intuition specifically applies to our intuitive understanding within the context of the digital world.

3. Can I develop my digital intuition? Absolutely. Just like other skills, digital intuition can be nurtured and enhanced. Various exercises, such as mindful media consumption, can help in honing your digital intuition.

4. How can I tell if my intuition is accurate? While it may not be foolproof, repeated patterns, personal experiences, and outcomes can help validate your intuition over time. Intuition is often validated retrospectively.

5. Is intuition only about 'gut feelings'? While 'gut feelings' can be a form of intuition, intuition is more expansive. It can manifest as a sudden insight, a hunch, a strong pull towards or against something, or even a prophetic dream.

6. Does digital intuition mean predicting the outcome of online events? Not necessarily. Digital intuition might guide you towards fruitful online interactions, assist in decision-making, or help navigate digital complexities, but it's not about predicting specific outcomes.

7. How does the digital age affect our intuition? The digital age influences our intuition by offering an unprecedented volume of information, and varied contexts. It can either overwhelm and cloud our intuitive sense or hone it, based on how we engage with the digital world.

8. Can digital intuition help me professionally? Yes. Digital intuition can aid in decision-making, understanding digital trends, handling online communications, and more, proving beneficial across different professions.

9. Is digital intuition a form of artificial intelligence? No, digital intuition is a human capability, not a machine function. However, AI's predictive modeling might appear intuitive, it's based on algorithms and data analysis, not innate human perception.

10. What are ethical considerations for digital intuition? Ethical considerations include respecting privacy and consent, recognizing the implications of digital divide, and understanding that while intuition can guide us, it should not be used to stereotype or discriminate.

11. Does everyone have digital intuition? Everyone has the potential to develop digital intuition, just as we all possess the capability to develop traditional intuition. However, it might be more refined in some individuals based on their digital exposure and practices.

12. Is digital intuition infallible? No. While digital intuition can provide useful insights, it's not always right. It's important to balance intuitive knowledge with rational analysis.

13. How can I teach my kids about digital intuition? By encouraging mindful use of digital technology, fostering open conversations about their online experiences, and guiding them towards recognising their feelings and hunches related to digital interactions.

14. Can digital intuition help with online safety? Yes, it can. Listening to your intuition can help identify potential red flags or unsafe situations in the digital space.

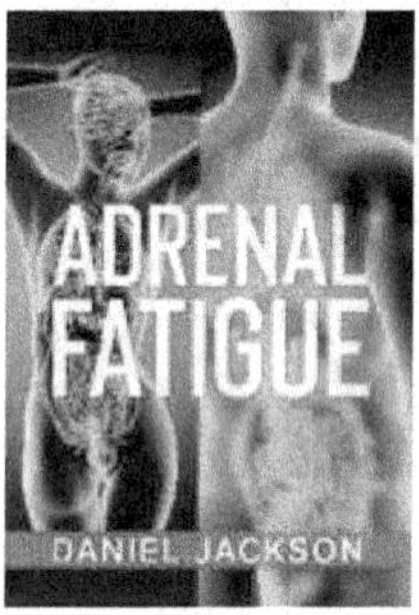

Take a look at more great books available from Rockwood Publishing

... some for FREE!

Just visit the link below:

rockwoodpublishing.co.uk

amazon kindle amazon

kobo iBooks Rockwood Publishing nook BARNES&NOBLE BOOKSELLERS www.bn.com

Published by Rockwood Publishing 2023

to the subject matter covered. The information included in this book has been compiled to give an overview of the subject(s) and detail some of the symptoms, treatments etc. that are available to people with this condition. It is not intended to give medical advice. For a firm diagnosis of your condition, and for a treatment plan suitable for you, you should consult your doctor or consultant. The writer of this book and the publisher are not responsible for any damages or negative consequences following any of the treatments or methods highlighted in this book. Website links are for informational purposes and should not be seen as a personal endorsement; the same applies to the products detailed in this book. The reader should also be aware that although the web links included were correct at the time of writing, they may become out of date in the future.

Disclaimers

The content contained within this book is for information and entertainment purposes only, and in no way purports to represent professional medical opinion. It should NOT be used as a substitute for expert advice, and you must consult with your designated health professional before acting upon any information contained herein or before undertaking any practice whose methodology is referred to in this book. The author is NOT a registered health professional and the text merely represents personal opinion, not medical fact. The author cannot be held responsible for the consequences of any action derived from the reading of this book, as the content is not based on diagnosis and subsequent regimen. It is the reader's responsibility to seek proper, professional medical advice from a registered health practitioner in connection with any material contained within this book.

Legal Disclaimer (part 1)

Nothing in this book should be construed as an attempt to diagnose, treat or cure. The information in this book is intended to be a community resource. The author takes no responsibility for any informational material or brochures produced using information

taken from this book. The author has endeavoured to ensure that all information is correct at the time of publication. This information, however, is subject to change without notice. The author makes no warranty with regard to the accuracy of any information and will not be liable for any errors or omissions. Any liability that arises as a result of this information is hereby excluded to the fullest extent allowed by law.
This information should not be used as a substitute for seeking independent professional advice.

Legal Disclaimer (part 2)

Disclaimer and Terms of Use:

a) i. In publishing this information, the author makes no representations concerning the efficacy, appropriateness or suitability of any products or treatments. Use this information at your own risk. The compiler is not a doctor and has no medical background or training.

ii. Statements and information regarding dietary supplements, books and any products mentioned have not been evaluated by any health authority and are not intended to diagnose, treat, cure or prevent any disease or health condition.

b) In view of the possibility of human error, neither the author nor any other party involved in providing this information, warrant that the information contained therein is in every respect accurate or complete and they are not responsible nor liable for any errors or omissions that may be found or for the results obtained from the use of such information. The entire risk as to use of this information is assumed by the user.

c) You are encouraged to consult other sources and confirm the information.

d) The information you access is provided “as is”. No warranty, expressed or implied, is given as to the accuracy, completeness or timeliness of any information herein, or for obtaining legal advice. To the fullest extent permissible pursuant to applicable law, neither the author nor any other parties who have been involved in the creation, preparation, printing, or delivering of this information assume responsibility for the completeness, accuracy, timeliness, errors or omissions of said information and assume no liability for any direct, incidental, consequential, indirect, or punitive damages as well as any circumstance for any complication, injuries, side effects or other medical accidents to person or property arising from or in connection with the use or reliance upon any information contained herein.

e) The author is not responsible for the contents of any linked site or any link contained in a linked site, or any changes or update to such sites. The inclusion of any link does not imply endorsement by the author. The author makes no representations or claims as to the quality, content and accuracy of the information, services, products, messages which may be provided by such resources, and specifically disclaims any warranties, including but not limited to implied or express warranties of merchantability or fitness for any particular usage, application or purpose.

f) The information provided is general in nature and is intended for educational and informational purposes only. It is not intended to replace or substitute the evaluation, judgment, diagnosis, and medical or preventative care of a physician, paediatrician, therapist and/or health care provider.

g) Any medical, nutritional, dietetic, therapeutic or other decisions, dosages, treatments or drug regimes should be made in consultation with a health care practitioner. Do not discontinue treatment or medication without first consulting your physician, clinician or therapist.

h) By reading this information, you signify your assent to these terms and conditions of use. If you do not agree to these terms and conditions of use, do not read/use this information. If any provision of these terms and conditions of use shall be determined to be unlawful, void or for any reason unenforceable, then that provision shall be deemed severable from this agreement and shall not affect the validity and enforceability of any remaining provisions.

i) The information, services, products, messages and other materials, individually and collectively, are provided with the understanding that the author is not engaged in rendering medical advice or recommendations.

j) The information and the terms of use are subject to change without notice. The material provided as is without warranty of any kind and may include inaccuracies and/or typographical errors. The author makes no representations about the suitability of this information for any purpose. The author disclaims all warranties with regard to this information, including all implied warranties, and in no event shall the author be held liable, resulting from, or in any way related to, the use of this information.

k) The unauthorized alteration of the content of this information is expressly prohibited. The author, its agents and representatives shall not be responsible for any claims, actions or damages which may arise on account of the unauthorized alteration of this information.

www.ingramcontent.com/pod-product-compliance
Lightning Source LLC
LaVergne TN
LVHW022048200926
848481LV00003B/825
* 9 7 9 8 2 2 3 6 8 7 9 5 5 *